Family Intervention

Family Intervention

Frank L. Picard

Parkside Publishing Corporation
205 W. Touhy Avenue
Park Ridge, Illinois 60068-5881

ISBN 0-942421-37-X

10 9 8 7 6 5 4 3 2 1

Printed in the United States of America

To my brothers, David and Roland.
Each died as a result of the disease and dysfunction
before they had an opportunity
to find the internal peace that I have found,
but they are at eternal peace.

Acknowledgments

W hen undertaking a work such as this it is difficult to know whom to thank, and especially how not to leave out people who contributed in a major way to its development. I have concluded that it is impossible to acknowledge all those who played a role. There are, however, certain individuals and institutions without whose guidance, mentoring, and acceptance this work would not have been possible.

The first on that list has to be the Heartview Foundation in Mandan, North Dakota. Heartview is one of the finest inpatient facilities for treatment of the disease of chemical dependency. It is the place that gave me hope in 1976. The people there not only gave me hope, they also helped me to believe in myself, to realize that I have value. That is where my spiritual awakening occurred and where my journey began. But it was only a beginning. Because I grew up in a highly dysfunctional home, much more healing was necessary. It is with a deep sense of gratitude that I thank the therapists who worked with me on ACoA (Adult Children of Alcoholics) issues long before that term was fashionable. To Russ, Al, Ray, Keith—each of you in your own way helped me to succeed and to learn how not to sabotage myself.

Next are the thousand families who over the years

have entrusted me with their interventions. From each of you, as families and as individuals, I have learned a great deal. From the very first interventions that were done in milking parlors and wheat fields in North Dakota to the interventions that occurred in the board rooms of major corporations, all of you have taught me that each intervention, each alcoholic, and each family is the same even while each individual, each family, and each situation is unique. Your trust and gentle teaching are gratefully acknowledged.

I would also like to acknowledge the interventionists around the country who perform the most important and difficult task in this field: getting patients to acknowledge their need. So for those of you who have been doing interventions in silence and with minimal recognition, know that your contribution is immense.

Finally, I offer special thanks to my family. My sons, Jim and Bob, provided much support. Their "You can do it, Dad" attitude has helped keep me going. The unwavering support, patience, encouragement, and loyalty of my wife, Pat, have been a source of strength. Her patience with Mac, the computer, as she transcribed this work and her patience with me as I struggled to stick with the task of writing make a mere thank-you seem quite inadequate.

Contents

Introduction

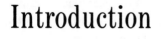

The theory that addiction to alcohol and other mood-altering substances is a disease has been accepted by the medical and psychiatric establishments since the early 50s. Nevertheless, we as a society still want to believe that solving the problems of addiction is as simple as "just saying no." As a professional who has long dealt with addiction, I see little evidence that either the general public or the addiction profession itself regards alcohol and other drug abuse as a disease.

Perhaps because health problems so often involve subtleties and intricacies not readily apparent to untrained eyes, public attitudes tend to ignore and avoid these complexities. But like the proverbial ostrich with its head in the sand, our culture depends on a one-dimensional, simplistic view of alcoholism and drug addiction that places us all at great risk.

Not only are we as a society failing to make headway in solving this problem, we are actually losing ground. The rates of increase in alcoholism and drug addiction are reaching what may be catastrophic levels. Moreover, addicts are not the only ones who are affected by this disease. Each addict directly affects the lives of the family members and friends who are close to him or her. These people also suffer lasting damage.

We are at a crossroads. We must come to grips with this disease and the toll it is taking on our people. Unless we can turn the corner in the next several years and begin reducing the number of alcoholics and addicts—and consequently the number of lives that are affected indirectly by addiction—we will have done irreparable damage to the fabric of our culture. The multigenerational dysfunction this epidemic will leave us with will include adults and young people handicapped by their own compulsive disorders, unable to bond, unable to form committed relationships, unable to experience personal success. This crisis is truly at the eleventh hour. It is not too late to reverse the trend, but simplistic answers and slogans will no longer suffice.

In an attempt to help the addict deal with his or her problem, the addict's family members and other loved ones often become involved in a process that we call "intervention." During this procedure, the most important people in the addict's life try to break through the addict's denial that he or she has a problem and that he or she needs help. Depending on how intervention is handled, it can either succeed in opening the door to treatment or can hinder the very recovery that it is meant to effect. How family members can contribute to a successful intervention is the subject of this book.

The concept of intervention is not new; it began with the founding of Alcoholics Anonymous in the 1930s. In 1980, Dr. Vernon Johnson's book, *I'll Quit Tomorrow,* clarified the concept of intervention and emphasized its importance in the treatment process.

Unfortunately, since then many people have come to accept the view that with a little bit of knowledge family members can "intervene on" their loved ones without professional guidance. But expecting family members to handle their own interventions in the complex disease of addiction is like expecting relatives to operate on loved ones who need surgery. More often than we would like to admit, the result is not intervention but rather a confrontation that further fractures the family system. If we are indeed dealing with a disease, then it is unrealistic to expect family members to be able to diagnose and interrupt the disease's process on their own. A little knowledge about intervention can be a dangerous thing.

This is a book about intervention, not confrontation. By explaining the complexities involved in intervention, this book can help the reader understand that simplistic approaches are not the answer. But most of all, this is a book about hope: hope for the alcoholic; hope for the drug addict; hope especially for family members, because they will realize that they no longer need to assess, diagnose, and begin the treatment process on their own.

Professionally guided intervention, in the hands of a trained practitioner who understands the subtleties and intricacies of this disease, is successful about 95 percent of the time. The more than one thousand successful interventions that I have had the privilege of guiding have taught me that intervention is not something separate from treatment but is rather the first step in treatment. How intervention is handled not only affects the outcome of treatment but also the extent to which the entire family is healed. This book is intended to help you find the hope needed to initiate the recovery process that so many families have successfully undertaken.

Though the material in this book speaks most directly to the family member of the chemically dependent person, it has been reviewed extensively by friends and colleagues in the treatment profession. Experts who had relied on confrontation as part of their day-to-day work with alcoholics, addicts, and their families have enthusiastically endorsed this work. Having something to offer other than confrontation, they report, has improved their counseling skills. I could not have hoped for more.

1

Addiction:
The Deadly Disease

While medical technology is advancing at an almost exponential pace, the disease of addiction remains vastly misunderstood, misdiagnosed, and mistreated. As a culture we are very quick to look with disdain on the drug addict. Cocaine, heroin, LSD, and marijuana are readily identifiable as drugs, and few dispute that they are harmful and addictive. Alcohol, however, is another matter.

In our culture today we are far more inclined to see alcohol as a beverage, not as the powerful drug it is. Alcohol is a drug, and alcoholism is an addiction to it. Our society's acceptance of nicotine as an addictive drug is far more widespread than our recognition and acceptance of alcohol as a drug, as evidenced by the amount of attention given by the Surgeon General and others to health-warning labels on products containing nicotine. Yet the side effects of alcohol are pervasive and extremely damaging.

Research tells us that as little as a few ounces of alcohol can cause irreparable damage to the fetus during pregnancy. A few ounces of alcohol in an adult affect motor skills and impair vision as well as hearing. Though research has provided us with much evidence about alcohol's addictive properties, we as a culture want to protect our belief that it is a beverage rather than a drug. Actors like Dean Martin and Foster Brooks have filled our concert halls and auditoriums with comedy performances about the results of drinking; we are much more likely to laugh at alcohol's effects than to be saddened by its destructive powers.

Medical research on alcoholism has identified multiple stages of the disease, from its very early onset to delirium tremens and death. But in spite of that research our society is still far more inclined to think of alcoholics as those who are on skid row and who suffer from DTs. Those who reach this stage are but a very small percentage of the alcoholics in our country. The rest die long before the disease has progressed that far.

The purpose of this book is not to debate whether or not alcoholism is a disease, nor to debate whether or not alcohol is a drug. Both are widely recognized and accepted facts among professionals. We as a culture, however, still lag far behind.

Alcohol as
an Addictive Drug

For a drug to be addictive, three criteria must be present:

1. It affects mood.
2. It affects the central nervous system.
3. The organism develops a tolerance to the drug.

Alcohol scores well on all three counts. Initially it acts as a euphoriant and lifts the mood of the consumer, then it acts as a sedative. It dramatically affects the central nervous system, causing the impairment of motor control, speech, hearing, and vision. And tolerance is identifiable simply by observing that with increased drinking experience an individual is able to handle more and more alcohol and outwardly show less effect.

In my practice I have developed the following criteria that can help you assess your own particular situation and can aid in your determination of whether or not you or your loved ones are suffering from the disease of alcoholism:

1. Hereditary factors
2. Loss of control
3. Failure to learn from experience

Though these criteria are not exhaustive, they provide a framework in which to evaluate your situation.

3

Hereditary Factors

The research of Goodwin, Lieber, and many others leaves no doubt that there is a genetic predisposition toward alcoholism. The genetic link is well established and is no longer debated. In over a dozen years of experience with addictions, I have not documented a single case in which we were able to rule out hereditary factors.

When families first look at this criterion, frequently their initial response is that no one they know of was an alcoholic. We must keep in mind that in looking at family history it is extremely rare to find the sort of definitive diagnosis that can only come about from treatment. Treatment has only been in existence for a few decades. Alcoholism has been accepted as a disease for more than forty years. Alcoholism has been listed as a cause of death on death certificates for an even shorter period of time.

To help determine hereditary factors I encourage you to look at the private discourse within the family. If you examine the patterns of conversation within a family with an alcohol problem you will probably hear the alcoholic referred to in statements like:

"Well, he always drank."
"He could hold his liquor."
"Rarely did she ever get out of control."
"He was a real boozer."
"She was a closet drinker."

Rather than seeking records of a specific diagnosis of alcoholism, look for the innuendos and the observations and reports of behavior.

4

It is not uncommon to find that such a family includes a generation of teetotalers. Those who have extreme views about the consumption of alcohol generally had very negative and painful experiences with alcohol while they were growing up. Also, it often happens that alcoholics are more or less excommunicated from their families. Look for siblings of the parents, or grandparents whom you rarely heard about and never visited and who seemed almost nonexistent. Often the family member who is estranged or separated from the family is the alcoholic no one wants to talk about.

Don't be afraid to ask questions about your family tree. I caution you, however, not to use the label alcoholic when making this inquiry. Ask about family members' drinking patterns and behavior rather than whether Uncle Louie was an alcoholic. Since, for many, the diagnosis of alcoholism means the presence of delirium tremens, asking whether or not Uncle Louie was an alcoholic will probably bring a negative response. If you can, ask about how he drank:

How frequently did he drink?
Were people worried about his drinking?
Did it cause him any problems?
Do you remember him trying to stop or control his drinking?

This type of inquiry into your family history is more apt to give you information on which to base your own assessment. Asking about alcoholics will frequently bring a one-word negative response.

The offspring of alcoholics have at least an even chance of becoming alcoholics if they start using alcohol. If hereditary factors are present on both sides of the family, the odds of developing this disease are even greater.

Loss of Control

Anyone who uses the drug alcohol to any extent is at some point going to have some negative experiences as a result of that usage. When an individual makes specific plans about how much he or she is going to drink on a particular occasion and then loses the ability to stick to those plans, that individual is experiencing a loss of control. An example of this would be a person who plans to stop for a beer after work and get home for dinner by seven, but ends up drinking much more than just that one beer and being driven home at two in the morning. This loss of control rarely occurs each time an alcoholic drinks, but is random and unpredictable.

When you are using this particular criterion to evaluate your own situation or that of your loved one, I encourage you to pay very little attention to the frequency with which a person drinks or the amount of alcohol consumed. Rather, pay attention to his or her words, and pay particular attention to results. Because of the negative consequences of drinking alcohol, an individual who continues to drink makes very specific plans to prevent the recurrence of such consequences. Listen to what people say when they tell you the adjustments they will make to prevent the same difficulties from recurring.

No person can experience a blackout without feeling a great deal of concern. No person can experience an arrest for driving under the influence without being alarmed. No person can see the pain in his or her spouse's or children's faces the next day without feeling remorse. As a result, such individuals will publicly or privately attempt to make a commitment to limit their consumption of alcohol to a lower level. If they are already well on the way to developing the disease, the failure of these plans will be accompanied by rationalizations and justifications; the addict will claim that each lapse was an exception due to special circumstances. As loved ones we are more inclined to pay attention to and believe these rationalizations and justifications than we are to look at specific behaviors and subsequent results.

There is a type of alcoholism in which the individual simply plans on a repeated basis to get intoxicated. That type is fairly rare, however, and is indicative of the late stage of alcoholism. During the early and middle stages, individuals frequently plan the opposite:

They plan to drink, not to cause problems.
They plan to be sociable, not to ruin the party.
They plan to have fun, not to be argumentative.
They plan to feel good, not to get sick.

Many alcoholics by nature are kind, caring, and sensitive people. They do not intentionally set out to inflict emotional pain on their loved ones. Listen to the plans they make concerning their drinking, in terms of both amount and frequency as well as behavior, and observe the results. If their alcohol consumption intermittently or continually exceeds the plan, chances are the your loved one has a drinking problem. Loss of control has very little to do with the amount a person drinks or with the frequency of drinking. It has to do with results.

Failure to
Learn from Experience

Because alcoholics generally are kind, sensitive, and caring, they are emotionally affected by the negative results of their drinking behavior. In the early stages of this disease they will express guilt, remorse, and regret as a result of the problems that occurred while they were drinking. The human capacity to learn and the sophistication of that learning separate humans from other animals. Physical and emotional pain are powerful teachers and motivators of change. Early on the alcoholic will experience considerable emotional pain as a result of his or her drinking behavior and will verbalize that pain. The guilt that the alcoholic feels, coupled with remorse, results in promises to cut down, control, or quit drinking. These promises are heartfelt and sincere, but they are not often kept.

To better understand this, let us look at a specific example. A year or so ago, in preparing for an intervention, a sixteen-year-old girl recounted the following situation: She was a star on her high-school basketball team and very much enjoyed her parents' attendance at the games. In her junior season, however, her father frequently showed up at the games intoxicated; throughout the games she could hear his voice in the stands over and above everyone else's, and she was continually embarrassed by his behavior. At one point his harassment of the referees and his frequent foul language brought her to tears in the locker room.

She and her teammates made it to the state tournament and progressed to the finals. Prior to the championship game she sat down with her father and had a heart-to-heart talk about his drinking and behavior at the games, and the effect it was having on her. She said, "Dad, I am

8

embarrassed by how you act, by how loud you are, and by your language." She told him about how she had cried in the locker room, about her coach's comments, and about the support her teammates had given her. She told her father how important this particular game was and how she wanted to be able to concentrate on her game, not to be constantly wondering whether he was going to be inappropriate again.

Her father felt the emotional pain that his daughter was in, and felt his own pain. He promised himself and his daughter that he would not drink before the game and that she did not have anything to worry about. Their heart-to-heart talk was so profound that both of them cried and embraced and expressed their love for one another. But when the night of the championship game came, there was Dad in the stands again, loud, vulgar, and intoxicated. Dad had lost the ability to learn from experience and to learn from the most powerful teacher of all: pain. This story is not at all unique.

The repetition of negative experiences in spite of best efforts and intentions is a powerful indicator of the presence of alcoholism. It indicates that, at least on occasion, the alcohol is in control and not the drinker. If the drinker were in control, he or she would have stuck to plans and kept commitments. Certainly alcoholics will attempt to rationalize and justify their behavior in order to make some sense out of what seems senseless, but it will be a vain attempt to relieve some guilt and remorse. Rationalization is a normal and natural defense mechanism that comes into play. I encourage you, however, not to get caught up in the rationalizations, but to listen to the commitments that were made and observe the results.

If in reviewing your particular situation or that of your

loved one you are able to identify any of the three criteria described above, then you can safely conclude that treatment and intervention are essential. For some, however, it is difficult to get away from the old idea that to be alcoholic you have to drink huge quantities on a daily basis. If you have reviewed the criteria and remain unconvinced that alcohol is a problem for you or your loved one, it can be helpful to look at the situation from another angle.

One way to gain a greater understanding of this disease is to look at the importance the addict places on his or her relationship with the drug itself. We only protect and defend what is important to us. When people constantly find ways to protect their right to drink and their time to drink, then their relationship with alcohol has taken on an abnormal level of importance. If a person's actions indicate that his or her relationship with alcohol has a higher priority than relationships with spouse, children, friends, or employer, that person has a serious drinking problem. In the case of our sixteen-year-old basketball star, her father's relationship with alcohol became more important to him than his relationship with her.

An individual who receives a driving-under-the-influence citation and then begins to drink and drive again is risking personal freedom to protect his or her relationship with alcohol. In most jurisdictions today a second conviction results in mandatory jail time. When people are willing to take that risk and all of its ramifications, including increased insurance costs, possible loss of the ability to get to and from work (and subsequently the ability to be gainfully employed), and public and private humiliation, this indicates very clearly that their relationship with alcohol has reached unhealthy proportions. If alcohol causes an individual to be willing to take repeated risks with health, employment, personal relationships, or freedom, he or she is indeed alcoholic, irrespective of the frequency with which this occurs.

Because the alcoholic has been stereotyped, the words alcoholic and alcoholism trigger a great deal of fear in both alcoholics and their loved ones. As a result a host of defense mechanisms come to the fore. Because of the stereotypes and the resultant fear, both alcoholics and their loved ones quickly begin trying to rationalize and justify the alcoholic's behavior. When those rationalizations and justifications begin to fail, silence occurs:

> What was talked about during the early stages of this disease now becomes a family secret.
> We protect the alcoholic from children, from employers, from their extended families, and from themselves.
> We try to control situations and circumstances, even the amount drunk.
> Most of all, we stop talking.

We stop talking about what's happening and what the results are, and the conspiracy of silence contributes to the disease. When our efforts at control fail we begin to doubt our belief in ourselves and our belief that a problem exists. The denial of the family becomes as strong as the denial of the alcoholic if left unchecked.

Being an alcoholic family has been likened to having an elephant in your living room. Everyone walks around it. Everyone pretends they don't see it. And certainly everyone pretends the elephant does not have an odor. The difficulty with having an elephant in the living room is that when a stranger walks into the house, he or she immediately sees the elephant and readily identifies it. The infrequent visitor will say, "Hey, this looks like an elephant." And you as a family will quickly deny that there is an elephant in your living room; you cannot for the life of you understand what is being seen or referred to. If the alcoholic is to be successfully treated, intervention must take place before the denial system of the family weaves such an entangled web that elephants are no longer visible.

The Harmful Relationship

For those who get trapped in a progressive dependency on mood-altering drugs, a powerful relationship with the drug develops. It is this relationship that becomes most difficult for the family to understand and accept. For the person who is developing a dependent relationship with alcohol or other drugs, there is a continuous increase in the importance of that relationship. Needs are met that the addict is unable to meet in any other way. A powerful bond is created.

For the chemically dependent husband who used to think of how nice it was to be on the way home to see his partner and enjoy a relaxing evening with his family, thoughts shift from the joy of seeing his family to the joy of the first drink, to how nice it will be to get home and to have that first beer or glass of wine or martini. After a while he begins to believe that the first, second, or third drink can pick him up, make him feel relaxed, make him feel okay, better than anything else ever has.

Alcoholics long for an embrace, but not an embrace of loved ones. They long to embrace a glass, to hear the sound of ice cubes, and feel the relief that comes from that first taste of their drug of choice. Those trapped in the web of addiction are having in essence a socially acceptable affair. When they are down, their relationship picks them up; when they are unable to relax, their relationship helps them relax; when they are unable to sleep, it helps them sleep. For those persons harmfully involved with chemicals, that first use of the mood-altering substance sends a sensation of warmth throughout their body. No marital, family, or employer relationship can provide that.

If you as a spouse or family member of a chemically dependent person feel as if you are playing second fiddle to the chemical, then there is a good chance that you are. To help you evaluate whether or not the person you are concerned about has developed a harmful relationship with chemicals, ask yourself what kinds of risks this individual is willing to take to protect his or her relationship with the chemicals.

If the individual is repeatedly driving under the influence, it follows that he or she is willing to risk safety and potentially freedom to protect the relationship with the chemical. If to protect one's relationship with a substance one is willing to risk life and limb as well as loss of freedom, the relationship has become pathological. If an individual is willing to drive while intoxicated with his or her family in the vehicle, he or she is willing to risk the safety of his or her loved ones to protect his or her relationship with alcohol.

Another area of risk-taking behavior involves alcoholics' relationships with their physicians. When people lie to their physicians about the amount of alcohol they consume, or when their physicians show concern about their drinking but they continue to drink, those individuals are placing their health and life at risk to protect their addiction.

The extent of an alcoholic's abnormal risk-taking behavior only determines the stage of the disease. The fact that this behavior is present, even on an intermittent basis, is enough to indicate that the person is an alcoholic.

Though the addict places less value on relationships with spouse and family and at times may endanger them with risk-taking behavior, this does not mean that he or she no longer loves them. What it does indicate is impairment, and that every day the family's importance in the addict's life will decrease while the importance of the chemical increases. This happens because the addict needs the chemical, not because he or she wants it.

Robert and Mary McAuliffe have developed a tool for diagnosis that centers around the importance of the drug relationship. In their book *Essentials for the Diagnosis of Chemical Dependency* they define psychological dependence as "an irrational need, caused by a person's committed drug relationship to rely on the ingestion of mood-altering chemicals in expectation of achieving rewarding psycho-physical experiences, or more concretely, in order to achieve welcome changes of feelings, moods and mind."* The following questions can help you assess the situation further.

1. How prominent is the presence of alcohol or drugs?
2. Does its presence appear secretive or pronounced?
3. Does the individual find ways to consume alcohol or other chemicals in an isolated or solitary way?

---

*McAuliffe, Robert, and Mary McAuliffe, *Essentials for the Diagnosis of Chemical Dependency, Volume 2* (Minneapolis, Minnesota: The American Chemical Dependency Society, 1975), p. 18.

4. Does the individual seem to manipulate circumstances and create opportunities to participate in events where known consumption will be occurring?
5. Is the individual avoiding health-warning labels and drinking in spite of being advised not to use alcohol as medication?
6. Is there a personality change that occurs with the ingestion of chemicals?
7. Is there a mood change that occurs?
8. Does it appear that the individual manipulates lifestyles or relationships with significant others to make continued use possible?
9. Is there repeated intoxication?
10. Has interest in other activities and pursuits diminished as the level of consumption has increased?
11. When the time of the individual's first drink has been delayed, does he or she appear to be uneasy, restless, or agitated?
12. Does the individual become hostile if, for whatever reason, that delay or obstruction of the normal drinking time is increased?
13. Is there a pattern of rapid ingestion of the first couple of drinks?
14. If you love someone who is harmfully involved with alcohol or drugs, have you at times felt:
    Frustrated?
    Angry?
    Rejected?
    Confused?
    Frightened?
    Worried?
    Replaced?

Ignored?

Second-class?

Discounted?

Or a host of many other unpleasant feelings?

15. In response to the situation, have you:

Adjusted?

Cajoled?

Pleaded?

Begged?

Forgiven?

Promised?

Readjusted?

Blamed yourself?

Blamed others?

Ignored?

Pretended?

Covered up?

Lied?

Threatened?

Prayed?

Or made a host of other responses normal for a loved one of a chemically dependent person?

If all of this sounds way too familiar, then chances are you are involved with someone dependent on alcohol or other drugs. I encourage you to stop trying to understand this rationally, because you are dealing with an irrational dependence and relationship. Commit yourself to seeking help so you can assist in the disruption of the harmful drug relationship and be a party to healing rather than enabling it to continue.

A True Disease

Practitioners of medicine have accepted the fact that alcoholism is a disease. They were able to do this because it had identifiable symptoms, an identifiable progression, an identifiable treatment, and, if left untreated, a predictable progression toward death. For purposes of diagnosis the progression has been divided into these stages:

Early or prodomal phase
Middle or crucial stage
Late or chronic stage

The following symptoms are visible in the early or prodomal stage of the disease:

Occasional relief drinking
The first blackout
Occasional sneaking of drinks
An increase in tolerance, i.e., the ability to handle
more alcohol before the effects show
Gulping of the first drink
An urgency about the first drink
Feelings of guilt
Drinking to relieve stress or anxiety
Avoidance of discussion of drinking

The middle or crucial stage of the disease is characterized by these symptoms:

Drinking accompanied by excuses
A show of remorse
Increased grandiosity
Increase in blackouts

17

Increase in promises and resolutions followed by increased failure in carrying them out
Loss of interest in others
Changing of friends
Changing of family habits
Change in drinking pattern
Attempts to stop drinking
Drinking earlier in the day, especially on weekends
Change of jobs, change of residence
Social engagements missed or canceled
Absence or tardiness at work

The chronic or late stage of the disease carries these symptoms:

Decrease in tolerance
Physical deterioration
Flushed face, broken blood vessels in the nose
Elevated liver enzymes
Moral deterioration
Drinking with inferiors
Change in drinking locations to inferior taverns
First bender
Onset of lengthy periods of intoxication
Impaired thinking
Loss of job
Vague spiritual desires
Morning tremors
Obsession with drinking
Ineffectiveness of alibis, excuses, and rationalizations
Permanent brain damage
Permanent insanity or death

Historically, treatment professionals and the medical community, as well as society at large, believed that nothing could be done for the alcoholic until he or she hit bottom. But as you can see from the preceding list, the symptoms of the late stage of alcoholism include permanent brain damage, permanent insanity, and death. If we wait until people hit bottom before intervening, then only a small percentage of those affected will be helped; hitting bottom is, for the most part, terminal.

The disease of addiction is no different from any other disease. Any disease is more treatable if treatment is begun at an early stage. Early treatment is easier and less costly, and it has a higher success rate. The same is true for the disease of addiction. If treatment begins earlier, it tends to be more successful because there is less denial present; the patient is less defensive and more amenable to treatment. In addition, the patient has suffered less physical damage. Unfortunately, many still want to wait until the patient is terminally ill before calling the ambulance.

Multiple Addictions

Alcohol is our oldest drug and still the most popular. In the United States, however, we believe that if a little is good then more has to be better. As a result we have developed significant problems with alcohol and drugs in our society. And today, the majority of people under the age of thirty-five entering treatment facilities are addicted to more than one substance. Let's review those other substances and the symptomatology (the symptom complex of a disease) surrounding them.

19

Cocaine

Cocaine is not new, nor is its use. It is known to have been used centuries ago by Latin American Indians, who chewed the leaf of the coca plant as part of their religious ceremonies. Sigmund Freud reportedly experimented with cocaine, and there are those who say he did far more than experiment. Medically, cocaine is occasionally used for certain types of nasal and oral surgeries. Primarily, however, it is an illegal street drug.

Once an infrequently used substance, cocaine gradually increased in usage until it became the drug of choice of the rich and eventually achieved its current mass popularity. In spite of the well-publicized deaths of people like John Belushi, Lenny Bias, and others, its popularity has not waned. In his book *800-Cocaine*, Dr. Mark Gold states that there are 5,000 new first-time users of cocaine per day in the United States. That adds up to 150,000 first-time users per month, and nearly 2 million per year.

Cocaine is extremely addicting. Initial use causes a tremendous rush of euphoria, immediately banishes fatigue, removes hunger, and causes increased sexual arousal and a sense of omnipotence. This initial experience can be so powerful that some are addicted from the very first time they experiment with the drug. Because it is impossible to know how pure the cocaine is or what substances were used to decrease the purity of the cocaine, death can result upon first usage. *There is no such thing as safe recreational use of cocaine.*

Though cocaine is no longer limited to the upper class and the rich, it remains a relatively expensive drug; many of those addicted to cocaine cannot afford to be. Thus it is common for cocaine addicts to become cocaine dealers in order to help cover the cost of addiction. The moral deterioration that occurs in the cocaine addict is far more significant than it is in the alcoholic. Users go from despising dealers to being dealers, from despising addicts to being addicts. Because cocaine has a psychosexual effect, users frequently get involved in sexual activity not previously a part of their repertoire. Because they are involved with a drug they cannot afford, they often steal from their family or pawn their own or their family's valuables. As the addiction progresses and behavior deteriorates, the risks that individuals take increase. They place themselves in dangerous situations and become secretive, paranoid, and protective.

One of the more difficult aspects for families to comprehend about cocaine addiction is the strength of the bond between the addict and the dealer. Many cocaine addicts elevate the status of their supplier to that of a god. They believe the dealer can do no wrong, that the dealer is their best friend, that the dealer is one of the few people who really care about them. These addicts will defend and protect the dealer, lie for him or her, cover up for him or her, and often will enter treatment only if there is an agreement that they don't have to say anything about their dealer.

You as a family member or friend may not see all of the hidden side effects of cocaine addiction, but generally you will be able to observe:

1. Financial irregularities and difficulties
2. Attitudinal and behavioral changes
3. Extreme changes in sleeping habits such as staying up all night and sleeping long hours during the day
4. Nosebleeds

5. Sore throat
6. Sniffles
7. Sinus problems
8. Rubbing of nose
9. Decreased interest in personal health and hygiene
10. Phone callers who leave no messages
11. Phone calls at odd hours
12. Change in peer group
13. Paranoia characterized by irrational fears
14. Irritability
15. Compulsive behaviors like tapping or jiggling of feet, hair combing, tie straightening, buttoning or unbuttoning
16. Increased use of alcohol or another drug
17. Unexplained absences
18. Cash withdrawals from the bank of $25, $50, or $100
19. Lying about finances

Rarely do people abuse cocaine on a regular basis without also abusing another drug. The most frequent drug of choice for the cocaine addict to abuse simultaneously is alcohol. Marijuana abuse, however, is also prevalent. Because of the dual abuse and dual dependence, the strategy of intervention must often be quite complex.

As the abuse and addiction increase, symptoms become progressively worse. Paranoid thoughts can eventually become delusions, including auditory, visual, olfactory, and tactile hallucinations. Addicts may be aware that their paranoid symptoms are not real and have enough self-control not to act on them, but they will remain hypervigilant, constantly checking their environment. This makes the addict extremely unpredictable.

It is important to remember these facts about cocaine:

1. It is highly addictive.
2. It is extremely dangerous, and major psychiatric and physical problems, including death, can occur from the initial usage.
3. Addiction progresses rapidly.
4. Intervention is difficult.
5. The longer one waits before intervention, the poorer the prognosis.

Marijuana

Perhaps no drug today is shrouded in more misinformation than marijuana. Many still believe it is nonaddictive and harmless. Neither belief is correct. A drug is addictive if it meets the following criteria:

1. It affects mood.
2. It affects the central nervous system.
3. The organism develops a tolerance to the drug.

Like alcohol and cocaine, marijuana meets all three criteria. Because its active ingredient, THC, is stored in fatty tissue, much of it remains in brain tissue for a prolonged period of time. As a result of its absorption into brain tissue, it affects the following functions:

1. Comprehension
2. Memory
3. Sleep
4. Emotions
5. Coordination
6. Vision

7. Blood pressure
8. Heart rate
9. Brain waves

Since reproductive organs contain a high percentage of fatty tissue, marijuana also has an adverse effect on the testosterone level in both men and women, decreasing it in males and increasing it in females. It reduces the number of sperm and may even alter the chromosomes of reproductive cells, thereby creating birth defects in offspring. If marijuana is used during pregnancy there is an increase in the mortality rate and in the number of birth defects. In addition, THC is passed on to babies through breast milk. Clearly marijuana is not only addictive but also highly dangerous. If you are concerned about a loved one's potential marijuana abuse, look for the following symptoms:

1. A change from active participation in family life to passive withdrawal, not only from the family but from normal interests
2. A decline in the quality of performance on the job or at school
3. Alienation from family and friends and a lack of consideration for the feelings and ideas of others
4. Chronic or frequent redness of the eyes
5. Decline in personal hygiene
6. An increased level of defensiveness when mild restrictions are experienced or observations are offered
7. Neglect of family responsibilities
8. A change in weight
9. Unexplained secretive phone calls
10. A change in peer group

The marijuana available today on the streets has a THC content anywhere from three to sixteen times greater than the THC content in the marijuana available in the 1960s. Because the marijuana grower is generally more concerned with making money than with the health of others, the varieties of marijuana grown today are often treated with pesticides, causing even greater toxicity and more unpredictable results and side effects. These are the important facts to remember about marijuana:

1. Its potency is much higher than it used to be.
2. It is highly addictive.
3. It causes physical damage, and the damage is greatest in the bodily organs that contain fatty tissue.
4. The individual often is simultaneously using another substance.
5. Recovery from the addiction is slow.
6. It takes years to regain normal brain function and alertness.
7. Its use is illegal, and addicts are often involved in other illegal activities, including dealing.

Other Addictive Substances

Many other drugs are abused besides alcohol, cocaine, and marijuana. Their degree of use varies considerably, depending on location. In the inner city the use and abuse of street-manufactured methamphetamine, a highly dangerous drug that is snorted or used intravenously, is increasing at an alarming rate. The use of hallucinogens such as LSD and Angel Dust is again on the increase in other areas.

In addition to street drugs, a wide variety of highly addictive pharmaceutical preparations are abused. All tranquilizers have addictive properties. Narcotics and synthetic narcotic pain relievers are addictive and very frequently abused. Prescription drugs such as Valium are also used frequently in conjunction with alcohol. Watch for the following signs if you are concerned about a loved one's use of prescription drugs:

1. Ignoring health-warning labels regarding the use of alcohol
2. Finishing the prescription before the normal time
3. Calling the doctor for refills
4. Seeing more than one physician and receiving similar prescriptions from all of them

The combination of alcohol and prescription drugs can be deadly. A drink plus a pill can have four to eight times the effect of one pill or drink alone.

Worksheet

The following is a worksheet to help you accept and understand whether or not a problem exists.

1. What evidence is there of a genetic link?

Parents_____

_____

_____

Grandparents⎽⎽⎽⎽⎽⎽⎽⎽⎽⎽⎽⎽⎽⎽⎽⎽⎽⎽⎽⎽⎽⎽⎽⎽⎽⎽⎽

⎽⎽⎽⎽⎽⎽⎽⎽⎽⎽⎽⎽⎽⎽⎽⎽⎽⎽⎽⎽⎽⎽⎽⎽⎽⎽⎽⎽⎽⎽⎽⎽⎽⎽⎽⎽⎽⎽

⎽⎽⎽⎽⎽⎽⎽⎽⎽⎽⎽⎽⎽⎽⎽⎽⎽⎽⎽⎽⎽⎽⎽⎽⎽⎽⎽⎽⎽⎽⎽⎽⎽⎽⎽⎽⎽⎽

Aunts⎽⎽⎽⎽⎽⎽⎽⎽⎽⎽⎽⎽⎽⎽⎽⎽⎽⎽⎽⎽⎽⎽⎽⎽⎽⎽⎽⎽⎽⎽⎽

⎽⎽⎽⎽⎽⎽⎽⎽⎽⎽⎽⎽⎽⎽⎽⎽⎽⎽⎽⎽⎽⎽⎽⎽⎽⎽⎽⎽⎽⎽⎽⎽⎽⎽⎽⎽⎽⎽

⎽⎽⎽⎽⎽⎽⎽⎽⎽⎽⎽⎽⎽⎽⎽⎽⎽⎽⎽⎽⎽⎽⎽⎽⎽⎽⎽⎽⎽⎽⎽⎽⎽⎽⎽⎽⎽⎽

Uncles⎽⎽⎽⎽⎽⎽⎽⎽⎽⎽⎽⎽⎽⎽⎽⎽⎽⎽⎽⎽⎽⎽⎽⎽⎽⎽⎽⎽⎽

⎽⎽⎽⎽⎽⎽⎽⎽⎽⎽⎽⎽⎽⎽⎽⎽⎽⎽⎽⎽⎽⎽⎽⎽⎽⎽⎽⎽⎽⎽⎽⎽⎽⎽⎽⎽⎽⎽

⎽⎽⎽⎽⎽⎽⎽⎽⎽⎽⎽⎽⎽⎽⎽⎽⎽⎽⎽⎽⎽⎽⎽⎽⎽⎽⎽⎽⎽⎽⎽⎽⎽⎽⎽⎽⎽⎽

2. What evidence is there of a loss of control?

   Cite times when the outcome was different from the plan.

   ⎽⎽⎽⎽⎽⎽⎽⎽⎽⎽⎽⎽⎽⎽⎽⎽⎽⎽⎽⎽⎽⎽⎽⎽⎽⎽⎽⎽⎽⎽⎽⎽⎽⎽⎽⎽

   ⎽⎽⎽⎽⎽⎽⎽⎽⎽⎽⎽⎽⎽⎽⎽⎽⎽⎽⎽⎽⎽⎽⎽⎽⎽⎽⎽⎽⎽⎽⎽⎽⎽⎽⎽⎽

   ⎽⎽⎽⎽⎽⎽⎽⎽⎽⎽⎽⎽⎽⎽⎽⎽⎽⎽⎽⎽⎽⎽⎽⎽⎽⎽⎽⎽⎽⎽⎽⎽⎽⎽⎽⎽

   ⎽⎽⎽⎽⎽⎽⎽⎽⎽⎽⎽⎽⎽⎽⎽⎽⎽⎽⎽⎽⎽⎽⎽⎽⎽⎽⎽⎽⎽⎽⎽⎽⎽⎽⎽⎽

   ⎽⎽⎽⎽⎽⎽⎽⎽⎽⎽⎽⎽⎽⎽⎽⎽⎽⎽⎽⎽⎽⎽⎽⎽⎽⎽⎽⎽⎽⎽⎽⎽⎽⎽⎽⎽

   Cite commitments made that were sincere but not kept.

   ⎽⎽⎽⎽⎽⎽⎽⎽⎽⎽⎽⎽⎽⎽⎽⎽⎽⎽⎽⎽⎽⎽⎽⎽⎽⎽⎽⎽⎽⎽⎽⎽⎽⎽⎽⎽

_____

_____

_____

_____

Cite examples of failure to learn from painful experiences.

_____

_____

_____

_____

_____

2

The Development of Intervention

Just as there is much mythology and misunderstanding among the public about the disease of chemical dependency, the practice of intervention is also poorly understood. Although intervention in various forms has been practiced for many years, its application has not been as frequent or as effective as it might have been.

The first discussions of alcoholism as a disease and advocacy of intervention began in the early 1930s, when Alcoholics Anonymous was founded. One of the founders, Bill Wilson, made numerous visits to late-stage alcoholics in jails and hospitals to bring a message of hope. In his visits Wilson was able to share with them the symptoms of their disease and the pain it was causing them, and he offered an alternative to that pain. Though his approach was unstructured, Wilson was the first person to regularly put into practice the idea that we do not need to wait until the alcoholic or chemically dependent person comes to us to ask for help; the right thing to do is to go to them. (In spite of his view, many in Alcoholics Anonymous support groups object to intervention on the grounds that it doesn't allow people to hit bottom.)

The pioneer of structured intervention was Dr. Vernon Johnson of the Johnson Institute. He has described his work in two books, *I'll Quit Tomorrow* (1980) and *Intervention* (1986). Dr. Johnson's premise is very simple. It is that alcoholism is a disease that has identifiable symptoms of both a physical and an emotional nature and that the disease progresses in a continued downward spiral. If the disease is uninterrupted, the affected individual will ultimately deteriorate both mentally and physically. The end result is death. Dr. Johnson saw that our society's belief that we need to allow the chemically dependent person to hit bottom was insane. He knew we had to reach the alcoholic and chemically dependent person before that point was reached.

Dr. Johnson's pioneering work has made an immense contribution to this field. To understand intervention theory and how it has evolved, it is important to view its foundation. In *I'll Quit Tomorrow*, Dr. Johnson described a typical scene from an early type of family intervention. The family of an alcoholic physician had consulted a counselor to learn about the disease and how to intervene. All of the family members were asked to list the specific behaviors of their alcoholic father or husband that were causing the concern. Then they met with the alcoholic on their own. This was the scene as described by Dr. Johnson:

> The meeting was called at the doctor's office in a building he owned. It was his afternoon off,

and he was alone. The young clergyman came directly to the point: "Actually, we are here to talk to you, Dad, about our deep concern with what is happening. Since it is no doubt going to be painful, I'm going to start out by asking you to promise, please, to hear us out." His goal was to create the father's role as a listener and then to keep him in that role.

The father was furious. His eyes were blazing. He leapt to his feet and paced the floor. "If you think I'm going to listen to all that again, you've got another thing coming!" It was a tirade.

Gently, throughout the demonstration, the son persisted, "Sit down, Dad, sit down, please!" Finally, the father sat down and fairly shouted, "All right! I know what you're going to say, but go ahead and say it if it'll make you feel any better!"

The daughter reached into her pocket, pulled out a written list, and began timorously and fearfully, "Dad, I came home from school last Thursday with two girlfriends. We came in the front door making so much noise that we woke you up on the couch. You swore at my friends so, Dad, that I'm ashamed ever to bring them over again but I think you were so drunk that you can't remember that!"

This enraged him. He jumped to his feet and put his face six inches from hers. "After all I have done for you," he shouted, "you dare talk to me like that!" The daughter burst into tears.

The young clergyman intervened. "Dad, Dad,

please hear us out! Please!" Finally he quieted his father and asked his sister to continue. She went on with more such events, just as specific as the first, while he pretended not to listen.

Finally, he had to drop that pretense and started pushing her along. "That's twenty," he would interrupt her, as she started a new incident. "What's twenty-one?" This crazy game went on. Finally she was through.

The twenty-year-old son was next, and in a voice that trembled a bit he began quietly, "Dad, I know what you probably will do to me, but gosh, I've been worried to death, so I've got to tell it like it is. I'm your janitor in this building and I cleaned it thoroughly three weeks ago. A week later I found five empty Scotch bottles in the places I had cleaned the week before. You're drinking on the job, Dad!" The father tried to wipe him out with a glare, but remained silent. The young man continued through the descriptions of four or five equally specific incidents that had caused him concern. When he finished, the father's tone was menacing. "I'll take care of you, all right!" he said.

The wife was next, and she was so fearful of his reaction that she apologized at length for what she was about to do. "I suppose this is the end of us, but then I'm convinced it would be anyway." But she plunged in. "What really got me scared happened two weeks ago," she said, and then related the story of a summons he had received on a charge of assault with a deadly weapon. "He has a gun permit because of the narcotics in his bag. And in a drunken moment, he waved his pistol in the wrong face and is being sued."

At that point, the other three in the room all exclaimed, "Mom, we didn't know that! When did that happen?" She turned to the two of her children who had already spoken and said, "I didn't know most of the things you just told about either."

She continued with her list, and a few episodes later the father jumped to his feet and dashed from the room. The family sat in stunned silence. While they were wondering what to do next, back he came carrying a case of Scotch whiskey which he put at his wife's feet, exclaiming heatedly, "Okay! Okay! I get the point! You take that and get rid of it. I quit drinking!"

She was greatly relieved and obviously ready to stop, but the older son sat his father down gently, over loud protestations, and urged his mother on. Bewildered, she continued, and a few minutes later the father jumped up and disappeared again. This time he returned with four partly filled bottles, obviously from various hiding places. Again he placed them at his wife's feet. "You take those, too. Now I do quit!"

She waited until he sat down again and went on reading from her list. She came to one of the last items. "Last Tuesday," she said, "there was an emergency phone call for you. I had to say the doctor was out, and you were, too, on the couch. There was no way you could have answered that emergency, being as heavily under the influence as you were."

During the recounting of this incident, his whole demeanor changed. All the belligerence just melted away. His hands went over his face, with his elbows on his knees. It was clear that he was quietly crying.

"The patient died," his wife went on, "and I know what that cost you. I know your devotion to your patients over the last twenty-five years. I know your commitment to the Hippocratic oath. I know what that cost you." And she was finished.

The doctor went on quietly crying, but all of a sudden something hit him as he realized there was still one person in the room left to speak. This was almost the most poignant moment of all. He lowered his hands and looked at his clergyman son and shook his head as if to say, "You don't have to say anything." The respect and love they had for each other was apparent during this silent interchange.

The son nodded back at him, then broke the silence gently. "Yes, I do, Dad, I'm the one who arranged this afternoon."*

Though the process was difficult for this physician's family, the family was successful and their loved one did enter treatment. By lovingly confronting the alcoholic with the reality of the disease symptoms, they were able to initiate the recovery process.

*Johnson, Vernon, *I'll Quit Tomorrow* (New York: Harper & Row, 1980), pp. 51-3.

The use of Dr. Johnson's basic model of intervention has had an 80 percent rate of success at the Johnson Institute. For many, however, this method of intervention appears so scary and difficult that they are too afraid to try it. Today, advances in the field of intervention have made it possible to avoid the shouting matches characteristic of the old intervention method.

Dr. Johnson's work has had three important benefits. First, it helped destroy the myth that alcoholics and addicts will not change until they hit bottom. Second, it was empowering; it gave families a sense of hope that they could make a difference. Third, his pioneering efforts became the foundation for the work in the field of intervention that was to follow. Because of Dr. Johnson, hundreds of thousands of alcoholics and addicts are alive today.

There are seven basic guiding principles in Dr. Johnson's style of intervention, as outlined in *I'll Quit Tomorrow:*

1. Facts should be presented by significant persons in the addict's life.
2. These persons should describe specific events that have occurred or conditions that exist.
3. The tone of the confrontation should not be judgmental. Instead, interveners should show genuine respect and concern as they confront the addict with the truth of his or her situation.
4. Whenever possible, the evidence should be linked directly to the drinking or drug-using.
5. The evidence should be presented in explicit detail to give the addict a clear overall view of his or her behavior during a given period of time.

6. The purpose of the presentation of this material is to have the alcoholic see and accept enough reality about his or her condition so that, however grudgingly, he or she will accept help.
7. When that goal is achieved, the choices available to the interveners may be offered. For example: "Do you wish treatment center A or B?"

Although each of these seven points is essential to the intervention process, I have some specific concerns about Dr. Johnson's model of intervention:

1. An objective professional is not present.
2. It is far too scary for some families.
3. It is confrontational in nature.
4. Ultimatums are often needed.
5. Anger frequently results.

During the history and development of intervention, the words intervention and confrontation have frequently been used interchangeably. I believe they are two distinct concepts. It does not take therapeutic skill to confront; it does to intervene. Confrontation is not new to alcoholic families; they in fact may confront the alcoholic many times before considering intervention. Because of that history, they are often reluctant to attempt to confront the alcoholic again because they do not want to meet with failure once more. Nor do they want to have to deal with the anger that generally results from confrontations. Even the word confrontation tends to elicit feelings of fear, anxiety, and hurt. From the very outset of the intervention process it is best to eliminate this word from the vocabulary.

Families who do their own confrontation make the tacit

assumption that they are healthy and objective. They hope that at least one person in the family will remain detached enough to prevent the confrontation from deteriorating. But this assumption is often incorrect. The disease of chemical dependency is a family disease. Each member of the family and each person close to the alcoholic or drug addict is affected and infected by the same disease. Each family member needs treatment as much as the chemically dependent person (except for the need for detox), and each has developed his or her own denial system and false belief system.

To clarify why I believe that a family on its own lacks the objectivity to do an intervention, let us look at the dysfunctional roles that develop within a typical chemically dependent family system. In this section I have drawn on the work of Sharon Wegscheider-Cruse, Virginia Satir, Claudia Black, and others who have written extensively about the roles that develop within chemically dependent families.

The Chief Enabler. In the alcoholic and chemically dependent family the Chief Enabler serves an extremely important role. Chief Enablers work tirelessly and endlessly to keep the family system together. They continually take on increased responsibility for the health and welfare of the family, such as the managing of finances and other tasks that had been done jointly. They keep secrets about the addict's behavior from the children or from the extended family, and they apologize and cover up for that behavior. They work hard to keep things running smoothly, not to ruffle any feathers, and to avoid family conflicts or disagreements that the alcoholic or chemically dependent person might use as an excuse to drink or take drugs. They act as a shock absorber for the chemically dependent person. When the addict is about to experience the consequences of his or her disease, the Chief Enabler tries to block or cushion the blow.

Chief Enablers are the people closest to the alcoholic or addict. They scurry the children to their rooms so they won't see Dad or Mom intoxicated. They cancel social engagements so that friends or members of the extended family do not see the impairment. They manufacture excuses for behaviors. The progression of this enabling runs parallel to the progression of the disease. The more advanced the disease, the more the Chief Enabler loses objectivity and strengthens his or her own defense mechanisms.

The Family Hero. Another of the identifiable roles in the chemically dependent family system is that of the Family Hero. Often this is the oldest child. This individual works extremely hard; he or she is the straight-A student, the athlete, the one active in drama or debate, the one who receives academic and professional recognition. Frequently the Family Hero is also the family therapist. Attempting to console and comfort the Enabler, he or she becomes the Enabler's confidant. The Enabler and others outside the family system often reinforce the Family Hero in this role with such statements as, "I don't know what this family would do without you." Family Heroes play very necessary roles in dysfunctional families. Their achievements and successes give some badly needed self-esteem to the family as a whole.

Outwardly the Family Hero looks like a model person,

but inwardly he or she feels lonely, lost, hurt, and angry. In addition, he or she feels torn between loyalty to the chemically dependent person and loyalty to the Enabler. Often Family Heroes initiate the intervention. But again, because of the role they have been forced to play in their sick family systems, Family Heroes lack the objectivity to intervene on their own.

The Lost Child. This individual deals with the stress and turmoil caused by alcoholism and chemical dependency by slowly but steadily withdrawing into isolation. This is the child who spends time in his or her room alone, with few friends and only solitary activities. The Lost Child has learned to deal with the intermittent or continuous crises in the household by swallowing feelings, isolating, and withdrawing. These unhealthy coping mechanisms result from a fear of conflict and confrontation.

The Family Mascot. I enjoy listening to comedians, and I am struck by the number of comics whose routines consist of jokes about the family. I wonder how many grew up in dysfunctional families and learned to use humor to cope. Family Mascots are the ones in the family system who can find ways to laugh in moments of crisis and chaos. They use humor to relieve their own stress, anxiety, and fear. They also attempt to take care of other family members by making them laugh at what is occurring. Although humor covers up the Mascot's true feelings of pain and hurt, it also helps the family avoid dealing with the pain within the family system. The person playing this role lacks the objectivity to intervene. Interventions are very stressful; often the Family Mascot will make jokes at crucial points, thus unknowingly sabotaging the process.

The Scapegoat. The Scapegoat is that individual who frequently takes the blame for the family's dysfunction and "takes the heat off" the chemically dependent person. The so-called black sheep of the family acts out the family dysfunction, trying in a subconscious way to call attention to the sick family system. In adolescence, those in this role may get involved in drugs, teenage pregnancy, and multiple acts of delinquency. They are the individuals who get in the most trouble at school. Their role is essential to the dysfunctional family system because it provides a major excuse for the behavior of the alcoholic or chemically dependent person. Often the Chief Enabler and the Family Hero also depend upon the Scapegoat.

I know of no knowledgeable mental health or addictions professional who would deny that these roles develop and that the entire family system becomes affected and infected by the disease of addiction. If trained professionals now agree on this concept of the dysfunctional family system, then how can we expect families to be objective enough to do interventions on their own? Each individual within the family system needs guidance and support from a trained professional for intervention to be therapeutic.

Without that professional guidance, the likelihood is great that defense mechanisms and unhealthy coping skills will surface during the intervention and cause it to fail. The result is more family pain, more scapegoating and blaming, further fracturing of the family system, and a forcing of the family into an even deeper well of secrecy.

Even when a self-guided confrontation is successful and the prospective patient does enter treatment, serious problems may arise. Oftentimes the patient enters treatment with so much anger that the first several days of treatment are wasted in terms of any therapeutic benefit. The anger generated through the confrontation may take months to heal, and may cause family members a great deal of fear and heightened anxiety. The family may be left wondering whether or not they did the right thing.

A professionally trained interventionist working with the family system throughout the preintervention, the intervention itself, and the postintervention can prevent these problems from occurring. In addition, a professionally guided intervention by a properly trained clinician will take into account the disease and dysfunction of the entire family system. Rather than asking the families to overcome their defense mechanisms and dysfunction to confront the chemically dependent person on their own, the clinician will work with those defense mechanisms to help the families intervene rather than confront. Professionally trained interventionists can also help by:

Lowering the threshold of fear
Encouraging a sense of safety
Providing support
Supplying much-needed objectivity
Assisting each participant to move from a dysfunctional role to a role that involves healthier communication

The Family Secret and Family Shame. Another reason to seek professional help for intervention is to break the pattern of family secrets and family shame. No one person in the family system knows all of what is happening. Each person knows a little bit, but no one talks openly and honestly about what is occurring. Each member of the alcoholic or chemically dependent family system feels a sense of guilt and shame and is afraid to let anyone else know. In fact, each feels the same sense of guilt and shame that the alcoholic or chemically dependent person feels.

Going outside the family system for professional help breaks the family rule of secrecy and says that what has happened is not going to be hidden anymore. That act empowers the family to a considerable degree. It also gives the chemically dependent person or alcoholic permission to accept help in a way that does not often occur with self-run interventions, which tend to reinforce the secret. Having a professional present makes it easier for family members to say, "If everyone knows, I may as well face it."

Though confrontation can be very powerful and can elicit the results the family is looking for, it also can be frightening and risks aggravating the worst part of the disease, both for the addict and the family. If we truly intervene rather than confront, the power for change comes from love and from the heart and these negative effects are avoided.

The Avoidance of Pain

Each role we have outlined serves a purpose. Each role keeps the pathology of the system alive. Each role keeps the focus off the primary problem. Each role helps each individual avoid the pain he or she is feeling. Each individual in the addictive family system—the alcoholic, the significant other, the mascot, the scapegoat, the lost child, the family hero—hurts very deeply.

If you doubt that pain, in yourself or your loved ones, I encourage you to go to an Al-Anon meeting and see the tears and feel the pain that comes from living with this disease. Go to an open meeting of Alcoholics Anonymous or Narcotics Anonymous and hear, see, and feel the pain of the alcoholics and addicts. See the pain that arises from the alcoholic's and addict's awareness that they used their disease to manipulate others. Hear the pain that results from near brushes with death. Feel the pain that results from the awareness of how much they trampled on the hearts of their loved ones. Go to a meeting of Adult Children of Alcoholics and listen to the adult child relate the pain of childhood experiences, missed events, abandonment, fear-ridden holidays, verbal violence, and the pain that arises from the confusion he or she feels. Then look in the mirror. All of that pain is your pain whether you are a parent or a spouse or a child.

But as you listen for the pain at an Al-Anon or Alcoholics Anonymous or Adult Children of Alcoholics meeting, so must you listen for the hope and the joy. Each person involved in those community-based support groups has a renewed sense of optimism and hope. They have gotten there by facing their problem, both within themselves and their family systems. By facing their individual situation they have also realized that they are not alone. Not only are they no longer feeling lonely but they are feeling a sense of real hope and are beaming with pride. They feel pride for they have faced life on life's terms. They have faced their fear and have walked through it. That sense of pride can only come from breaking through the multigenerational cycle of disease and dysfunction.

Hear them saying to themselves, Yes, I covered up; Yes, I pretended everything was fine; Yes, I was ashamed of this disease in my family system, but I stopped pretending, avoiding, and denying, and I broke through. As a result I can begin anew having healthy relationships and honest communication. From that breakthrough comes a sense of excitement, a sense of purpose, and a sense of hope for the first time.

The steps to achieving that are simple. The first step is acceptance. Accepting that addictive disease and all of its trappings are part of you and your family system. The second is to break the rule of the dysfunctional family and go outside the family to seek help. It has long been established that a family system is as sick as its secrets. By seeking help you have stopped keeping secrets. The third is to follow through. So take your fear in hand, read on, seek help, and follow through until treatment begins.

3

Understanding
Chemical Dependency

Those close to the chemically dependent person find it very difficult to understand and accept the changes occurring within that person. The often-erratic nature of those changes makes them not only confusing but easy to interpret as a lack of love and commitment.

It is possible, however, to understand the belief system and personality that evolves with the disease of chemical dependency. The more you can comprehend this belief system and personality, the more objective you will be about the disease. When you are able to see that the behavioral changes of the person you are close to are not aimed at you, when you can avoid taking them personally, you will be able to intervene much more successfully.

The A and B Sides of
the Personality

In order to understand the chemically dependent person in your life, it is helpful to think of his or her personality as having two sides: A and B. *A* represents the behaviors the person has developed as defense mechanisms; *B* is the basic core personality—that person's nature when he or she is not in the grip of the disease of chemical dependency.

A = The defense mechanisms developed by the chemically dependent

B = Core personality and beliefs

The B Side. Many chemically dependent people, by their very nature, are kind, sensitive, big-hearted, altruistic, loving, gentle, and caring. It is this core structure of their personality that makes coming to grips with the disease so difficult, both for them and those close to them. They are often the people who will go out of their way to help someone in need; the people who will find the most ways of saying "I love you." As the disease progresses, this kind, sensitive side of the person becomes more and more difficult to see as it becomes progressively obscured by defense mechanisms.

The A Side. The A side of the personality is where the defense mechanisms of the dependency are found. The chemically dependent person will deny, rationalize, justify, defend, and blame. And when all the other defenses fail, anger will surface and the person will simply tell you to mind your own damn business: "This is my life. What I do is up to me. You take care of you and I'll take care of me."

The extent to which these defense mechanisms are present depends solely on the stage of the disease. The more advanced the disease, the more these defense mechanisms and behavior will dominate the core personality. Defense mechanisms evolve to protect the psyche of the affected individual. They are there to protect that individual from feeling the overwhelming sense of guilt and shame that would come with facing the behavior and the symptoms of this disease head on. Defense mechanisms are neither good nor bad, but natural: difficult to understand and to cope with, but not bad.

A dictionary of psychological terminology defines a defense mechanism as "an involuntary or unconscious measure adopted by an individual to protect himself against the painful effect associated with some highly disagreeable situation, physical or mental, of frequent occurrence; it may be employed to cover a wide range of phenomena."* In other words, these mechanisms are not malicious or purposeful; they are not used deliberately to inflict emotional pain on you or other loved ones. Chemically dependent persons act and behave the way they do because they need to, not because they want to.

At this point I encourage you to get a notepad and pen and begin trying to get in touch with both sides of the person you are concerned about. With paper and pen in hand, first try to remember some of the times when the naturally kind, sensitive, and caring side of that person was present; jot down some notes that will help you recall these later on. Below is a list to help jog your memory. For each item listed, try to briefly identify a time when you were

*Drever, James, *A Dictionary of Psychology* (Middlesex, England: Penguin, 1952), p. 61.

aware of the B side of the chemically dependent person. Some of the items on the list may also trigger memories of the addictive side, but for now let's just stick with the core personality. What was it that this person did or said that showed the B side of his or her personality? Maybe it was nothing more than a look, a feeling, a touch.

Special moments in your relationship:
 Dating times
 Engagement
 Wedding day
 Honeymoon
 Special intimate talks
 Times when you felt especially close

Special times as parents:
 Pregnancy
 Childbirth
 Illnesses
 Special activities
 First report card
 Times when you talked about parenting, how it was going to be different, how it was going to be better
 Times you shared your hopes and dreams for your children
 Times with other children

Times when other people were in need:
 Neighbors
 Friends
 Deaths of neighbors or friends
 Illnesses of friends, neighbors, coworkers

If you are a child of someone who is chemically dependent, try to get in touch with some of the times you felt this parent cared: Christmas, a birthday, your first bicycle, first school play, first school concert, first date, first school dance. What did this person say or do that let you know you were loved and cared for?

If you are an employer, think about the person's behavior toward other employees, and his or her acts of kindness toward those experiencing difficulties. Remember examples of a willingness to help, a willingness to go out of the way, to do extra things, and to show commitment.

If you are a friend, remember the times when your friend has spoken lovingly of his or her spouse or children, or has been of aid and assistance to you.

Remember that if the disease of dependency has progressed very far, you may only be able to see his or her B side by looking at the past. The more the disease progresses, the less visible the core personality is and the further back in your memory you will need to look. Also be aware that sometimes it is initially difficult to remember the good in this person because your own hurt and anger are in the way. These feelings are as normal as the defense mechanisms of the chemically dependent person. Your interventionist will help you deal with that anger, which is your defense mechanism, so that you will be able to assist in the intervention. Don't try to swallow it and pretend it isn't there, and certainly don't get angry at yourself for feeling what is normal and natural.

It is very important to the intervention process that you develop an understanding of the chemically dependent person. It is equally important that you understand how this disease has affected you, and what defense mechanisms you have developed to cope with it. No one can be emotionally involved with a chemically dependent person without experiencing hurt. Because of the presence of the disease, the chances to deal with that hurt within the context of the relationship become infrequent and often nonexistent. The lack of such opportunity creates anger.

The environment created by the disease of chemical dependency does not allow us to deal with anger in a constructive way. Unresolved anger leads to repression, and then to denial and covering up. In fact, the closer one is to the chemically dependent person, the more susceptible one is to developing the same defense mechanisms as the chemically dependent person. For example, the spouse of the chemically dependent person can also develop the ability to rationalize, justify, defend, blame, and deny.

Keeping your pen and paper handy, now begin to identify some of the times when you have seen the A side of the person you are concerned about, the defense mechanisms that are a normal and natural part of this disease. Remember that those defense mechanisms are the ability to deny, rationalize, justify, defend, blame, and minimize one's behavior. If those fail, anger and rage ensue.

As you may recall, one of the identifying characteristics of this disease is the loss of control. This is demonstrated by an individual's inability to maintain a specific plan about his or her drinking or drug use. Try to remember the various times when the person made commitments regarding consumption of alcohol or drugs. The following list should be helpful.

Special occasions
Birthdays

Anniversaries
Having company for dinner
Family events
Children's events
Vacations

What was the commitment, what happened, and what defense mechanism surfaced? How did the alcoholic or chemically dependent person rationalize, justify, and defend the behavior and the consumption? What guilt, remorse, and regret were expressed? What promises about next time were made? If children are involved, think of times when they felt hurt, sad, scared, or embarrassed.

Try to remember specifics for each defense mechanism we have mentioned. Following are some common excuses:

I lost track of time.
I was just visiting.
I got too busy.
It doesn't happen very often.
It was a special occasion.
It's just wine.
It's just beer.

Who or what does the alcoholic or chemically dependent person blame: a hard day at work, lots of stress, lots of tension, the kids, you, the in-laws, the boss, a coworker, "someone" who spiked the drink, the weather? Remember that we are not doing this to be judgmental; we simply are trying to pinpoint the symptoms of the disease. Think of specific instances when the chemically dependent person tried to rationalize consumption and behavior, and think of particular excuses that were used:

I just had a few.
I hadn't eaten.
I had eaten.
I ate the wrong stuff.
I was tired.

Think of times when his or her anger surfaced and:

You feared for your safety
Things were broken
The children or you were abused

These exercises have probably helped you become aware that the personality of the one you are concerned about has two distinct sides. The closer you are to the person, the more the disease has progressed, and the longer you have been involved, the more your objectivity will be affected. Don't let that stop you, however. Seek assistance from your interventionist. If you have been close to the person for a long time, identifying both sides of this individual may take a considerable amount of time and energy. Continue to remind yourself that you are not dealing with right and wrong or good and bad, and that what is occurring is a normal and natural part of the disease process. The more we are able to get away from making a value judgment about what is occurring, the more able we are to intervene.

The Belief System of the Chemically Dependent Person

Besides developing certain defense mechanisms that affect their personalities, chemically dependent people also evolve an identifiable belief system. The belief system consists of four distinct components:

1. The knowledge that he or she has a problem.
2. The belief that others would not understand.
3. The belief that he or she would be rejected if others knew the extent of the problem.
4. The belief that his or her situation is unique.
5. I'm stuck—what's the use.

Let's look at each individual component of this belief system.

Knowledge of the Problem

Individuals will not necessarily use the terms "alcoholic," "drug addict," or "chemically dependent" in describing themselves, but they will indirectly reveal their awareness of the problem. For example, they may acknowledge inappropriate consumption and use the terms "problem drinker" and "alcohol abuser." Those close to the chemically dependent person may not notice these indications of awareness because they are very quickly followed by excuses and rationalizations of the behavior. Nevertheless, if you think back to the early stages of the disease, you will be able to identify several times when the individual admitted that what was occurring was indeed a problem.

The average person with whom I intervene has already in some way sought help on approximately three separate occasions. The difficulty is that these people do not seek specific help for their addiction; the untrained individuals or organizations they go to for help are unable to pick up the hints and cues that are given about the chemical dependency. Because the same belief system develops within the family, family members also will have sought help an average of three times before the intervention. They most commonly consult pastors, marriage counselors, or family physicians. In each such contact, hints and innuendos usually point to the true problem, but the untrained professional does not know how to read these cues and so is unable to assist in the way that is needed.

By the time of my intervention, the alcoholic or chemically dependent person, too, already will have talked to a friend, medical doctor, or counselor, and may even have called Alcoholics Anonymous or a treatment center. But each of those attempts turns into an effort on the part of the addict to prove that he or she is unique. Such attempts don't help individuals recognize the seriousness of their problem or request specific assistance for it. Treatment facilities and information and referral services on alcohol and drug abuse get numerous anonymous calls from individuals wanting information about "a friend." The more the disease progresses, the more the chemically dependent person seeks information to prove that he or she does not have the disease: "I know I have a problem, but . . ."

"You Don't Understand"

This component of the individual's belief system is quite sincere. In their heart of hearts the chemically dependent truly believe that others do not and would not understand. For, in fact, they themselves don't. They do not understand how they can make commitments and not follow through, how they can make plans and not stick to them, and how they can be kind, loving, and sensitive one day yet be angry, belligerent, and mean the next. "If I cannot understand my behavior and my lack of control, certainly others will not."

This belief is reinforced for the chemically dependent person by his or her interactions with others. How many times have you told yourself and your loved one that you don't understand? Even when the words aren't spoken, body language and facial expressions say it very loudly. That look of bewilderment conveys a clear meaning to the chemically dependent person.

"Others Will Not Accept Me"

As the disease progresses, self-esteem erodes. Many of the actions of chemically dependent people are known only to themselves. You may never have had an opportunity to observe them sneaking drinks, but they have observed themselves. As the disease progresses, their behavior becomes more and more secretive. The belief that no one could accept them if they knew the full picture becomes stronger and stronger. This belief can become so dominant that suicide becomes a viable option. The disease of chemical dependency breeds self-loathing, self-disgust, self-hatred, and shame.

The patterns of action and behavior that alcoholics and chemically dependent people develop are unacceptable even to themselves. Their lack of self-acceptance is then projected onto others and becomes a core part of the belief system. As the disease progresses, this belief grows stronger, yet it may be outwardly demonstrated less often.

"I'm Different, I'm Unique"

There are numerous ways in which the chemically dependent person demonstrates this aspect of the belief system. We see individuals redefining what it is that constitutes a problem. They explain why so-and-so has a problem and they don't. If they go to an A.A. meeting they come home armored with the differences they have noticed, not the similarities. From an evaluation they may grasp only the symptoms they don't have rather than those they do. Another aspect of this belief is that the person is convinced that there is nothing that can help his or her particular problem: "It works for other kinds of alcoholics and addicts, but it wouldn't work for me." Remember that we are dealing with a strong genetic component in the disease of chemical dependency. These individuals' image of an alcoholic or addict may be based on a parent or relative they swore they would never be like. Therefore, they focus on the differences between themselves and that image.

Naturally, the chemically dependent person will define a problem as something that he or she does not quite have.

As the disease progresses the definition of who it is that has a problem will continue to change:

From "people who drink and drive"
to "people who get more than one drunk-driving ticket"
From "someone who can't get home on time for dinner"
to "someone who is out all night"
From "an individual drinking out of control on an intermittent basis"
to "someone who is out of control every night"
From "someone who is out of control at home"
to "someone whose drinking or drug usage interferes with work"
From "people who have drug or alcohol problems at work"
to "people whose addiction causes severe physical impairment"

Continual redefinition of what constitutes a problem is quite common. It fits very well with the rest of the belief system: knowing that you have a problem but believing that no one would understand or accept you, believing that the problem you have is different and somehow unique, and therefore resorting to denial and hopelessness.

Belief System of the Family

The family of the alcoholic tends to develop the same belief system. How many times have you as a loved one said, "I know it's a problem but you don't understand"? How many times have you sincerely felt that neighbors, friends, or members of the extended family really do not understand, that they don't understand the stress and the pressure that your loved one is under? Certainly others would not understand what goes on behind closed doors.

Not only would they not understand, but certainly they could not accept the Jekyll and Hyde personalities you have seen. They couldn't understand or accept the sexual conflicts, the extramarital affairs, the impotence. And besides that, the situation you deal with really is different than most.

> He is not as bad as . . .
> She doesn't drink as much as . . .
> And besides that he is so good about . . .
> He's not at all like John or Mary.
> She's never missed work.
> He's never beaten me.
> She's never played around on me.

Try to get in touch with all the different ways you've tried to convince yourself and others that your situation truly is unique and different. Try to identify the different aspects of this disease that you felt others wouldn't understand or accept. Try to recognize how you have redefined what a problem is.

Just as this false belief system leads alcoholics and addicts to denial and hopelessness, the corresponding beliefs of those close to them have the same effect. Identify your own denial and hopelessness. Think of the times you've covered up by:

> Canceling a dinner party
> Declining invitations from neighbors, friends, and
>   extended family

Making excuses for inappropriate conduct
Giving excuses to the children
Blaming the children

Remember the times you told yourself or others that if certain things happened you would take some action, and then when those things did happen you did not follow through. Each time those events occurred you found ways to rationalize and justify your inaction. "It probably won't happen again. . . . Besides, he or she promised that it wouldn't happen again."

Remember that the belief system of the codependent is very similar to that of the chemically dependent person, though the behavior and defense mechanisms it triggers may differ. The more you can identify this belief system in yourself and develop an awareness of how it has played itself out in your life, the better prepared you will be to assist in an intervention.

As you develop insight into how you have accepted and acted on this belief system, I caution you to avoid blaming and criticizing yourself. Though that may tend to be your initial response, know that it is as normal and natural for you to have developed these beliefs as for the chemically dependent person to have done so. Do not look upon it as your failing but as part of the disease of codependency or para-alcoholism. The more you are able to view it as symptomatology rather than as personal failing, the more successful you will be. You are not the villain here and neither is the chemically dependent person. The villain is the substance and the disease. The more you understand how the disease progresses and how it has affected you, the more successful you will be.

4

The Intervention Process

To help you understand intervention, let me first share its essential components:

1. Bathing the chemically dependent person in love
2. Immersing that person in the reality of the problem—in words he or she can hear
3. Providing the person with viable solutions to the problem

The first, essential requirement of those who participate in intervention is that they truly care about the well-being of the addicted individual. A participant's genuine concern is vital to the success of an intervention—it is even more important than the afflicted person's full understanding of the disease. This concern needs to be expressed in a way that is not going to trigger the defense mechanisms of the chemically dependent person.

The second requirement of intervention participants is the ability to communicate reality in a way the chemically dependent person can understand. The English language can be either a powerful ally or our worst enemy in the intervention process. A successful intervention depends on our choice of words and how we use them. It is critically important that the chemically dependent person hear the reality of his or her impairment, but that reality needs to be communicated in a way he or she can hear, not in a way that would trigger (again) the defense mechanisms of this disease. If reality is communicated in anger, it will elicit anger. If it is communicated in the form of blame, it will result in blame. If it is communicated in such a way that the behavior is justified or excused, it will elicit justification and excuses. But if it is communicated concretely, accurately, and with compassion, it has the potential to elicit change.

The third essential requirement of those who intervene is that they provide viable solutions. The only solution available for someone affected with the disease of chemical dependency is intensive treatment. Stopping the use of a chemical enables treatment to occur, but stopping alone does not solve the chemical dependency problem. Only treatment can. The changing of jobs, relationships, or locales does not solve anything either; such changes are mere coping mechanisms that will ultimately fail.

To make the treatment solution viable one needs to eliminate the excuses for avoiding treatment. If time off from work is necessary, then arrange it. If financial assistance is necessary to afford treatment, then arrange it. Whatever may prevent an individual from accepting treatment needs to be dealt with openly and honestly so it is no longer an obstacle. Then when the intervention occurs the individual will be faced with the choice of accepting a viable solution or denying the love he or she has just received. Chemically dependent people, by the very nature of their disease, do some very dumb things, but they are not stupid. If not accepting treatment no longer has any viable rationale, they will see that the treatment is practicable and they will accept it.

In general, the intervention process must neutralize the primary belief system of the chemically dependent person and avoid triggering the defense mechanisms the disease presents.

The difference between intervention and confrontation is in the love that is shared. If that love is shared in a real way, confrontation can be avoided. I ask each participant in the intervention to write out word for word exactly what he or she is going to say so we can hear if that love will indeed be communicated.

Participants should begin by stating why they came to the intervention: because they care for the chemically dependent individual. Second, I ask them to share why they care. What is it about this person that they find endearing? What is good and decent about this person? What is special? Then I ask them to share a few specific examples of the person's admirable traits. In other words, what evidence is there that the B side of the personality exists? That kind, sensitive, caring, altruistic side?

When a participant begins with a statement of concern for the chemically dependent person, the communication is anchored in love, and concerns about the disease become more bearable. These concerns recognize the symptoms of the disease; they don't blame the afflicted individual.

Let me give you an example (names, situations, and locations have been changed). In a recent intervention a woman spoke eloquently of her chemically dependent friend's behavior and support during the time of her father's death. She talked about this friend being there with her at the hospital when her father died, of all the chores he took over during and after the funeral, and of his many kind words of support.

Not only did she speak of his kind and sensitive behavior; she also spoke about what his actions meant to her personally. The data sheet she prepared for the intervention went something like this: "John, I am here today because I care about you. We have been friends for a long time and that friendship has meant a great deal to me. I think especially of those times when you've been there as a friend for me, like the time last fall when my father died. You stayed with me at the hospital when Dad was dying because none of my family was able to be here. As my family began to arrive you went out of your way to extend a helping hand, to provide some housing, and to show that you cared in many ways. You came over and cut my lawn and offered many words of encouragement and support. It meant a great deal to me."

The First Step:
Seek Guidance

Once you as a family member or friend of an alcoholic or chemically dependent person have become concerned about the individual's level of involvement with alcohol or other drugs, it is time to seek help. I encourage you from the outset not to prejudge or predetermine whether intervention is a viable option, but simply to seek professional guidance and assistance to help determine the level of impairment and what treatment options are available, including intervention.

Because other members of the family system may not have the same level of understanding of the problem that you have, I encourage you to be cautious in terms of whom you invite to go with you, and to consider initially seeing a professional alone, there getting guidance on who other than yourself ought to be involved.

The purpose of the first session with a professionally trained interventionist is to allow that professional to evaluate the following:

1. Whether or not this individual is impaired
2. The degree of that impairment
3. The appropriateness of intervention
4. Who should be involved in intervention
5. Who else in the family system may have a similar problem
6. Who would be likely to sabotage the intervention

The trained professional usually can get a grasp of these things in an initial one-hour interview. Based upon the data you provide, he or she can begin to advise you on what approach to take and how to involve others who care for the chemically dependent person.

As a result of having sought professional help and having educated yourself about the problem, you need to be aware that you may be far ahead of other family members and others close to the chemically dependent individual. You have begun to understand that intervention need not mean confrontation and that it is not as frightening and scary as it first sounds. But you should also know that others may be lagging behind you. Your interventionist should guide you in your efforts to get others involved.

I encourage the person who is initiating the intervention process not to ask other people—family, friends, employer—to make a commitment to "intervention." Ask them only if they would come with you to get some education so they can decide for themselves whether or not they wish to be involved. If you ask them to commit to intervention, it is going to bring out their fear of confrontation, and they may either refuse to get involved or withdraw. By asking people in this way, you increase the likelihood that they will sabotage the process.

Once you have discussed these items in the first session with your interventionist, you should be ready to contact others to request them to become involved in the scheduling of the second meeting.

The Second Step: Meeting

At the second meeting with your interventionist are people who are important to the alcoholic or chemically dependent person: parents, children, friends, pastor, physician, employer. They are all there for the same reason: Each person cares about the well-being of the chemically dependent person. Each may have varying degrees of knowledge of the individual's impairment; the important factor is that they care. This session with the interventionist is designed in large part to provide this group with information upon which they can base a decision. They need to learn that they are dealing with a disease and that, barring intervention, the disease will progress. If they can reach the understanding that it is indeed a disease and that the individual does not have the wherewithal to deal with it alone, then not only will they feel free to participate in the intervention, but they will see that it is the only commonsense thing to do.

Once the education session is completed, each individual makes a personal decision about participating. Then a group consensus about the intervention is taken, and step three begins.

The Third Step:
Preparation, Rehearsal, Intervention

No one aspect of the intervention process can be viewed as more important than the other. Each is a building block. For the group to be able to prepare without fear, the two previous steps must have been completed.

To begin the intervention we ask each individual to state why he or she is participating: "John, I am here today because I care about you," or "Mary, I am here today because I love you."

In preparing the specific scripts to be utilized in the intervention, careful consideration is given to the defense mechanisms and belief system of the chemically dependent person. Part of the belief system of the chemically dependent person is that no one really does care and no one really does understand. To help neutralize that faulty belief system, each individual carefully prepares every word that will be said at the intervention.

To that end, we ask the members of the group to expound on why they care. We ask that they each share a brief paragraph or two about what is special about the chemically dependent person, what's good and decent about that person, what endears him or her to them. By anchoring the intervention process in love and in the B side of the personality structure of the chemically dependent person, we are able to move far away from confrontation. Throughout this preparation process the professionally trained interventionist is present to help the participants find the words that will be effective and nonthreatening.

For example, a seventeen-year-old son might phrase an aspect of the intervention in this way:

> Dad, there have been times when I have felt especially close to you. I don't know whether it was because I am your oldest son, but there are many times when I have felt like my relationship with you has been special.
>
> I remember feeling so proud when you coached my baseball team. I remember the pine-box derby, which was a father-and-son project, and even though the car we made didn't have a chance at winning, and might even have been a little ugly, we did it together. And you really made me feel included and special.

Notice the absence of anger, the absence of blame, and the presence of love. The first two key components of the intervention process are now present. One is the love.

The other is the data supporting that love. Simply stating that you love somebody (without the supporting data) will not be heard by the alcoholic or chemically dependent person. Their defense mechanisms have evolved to the point where those words by themselves lack believability. Details need to be provided. For family members and those close to the chemically dependent person to communicate love and to share supporting details and feelings, they will need to have received enough assistance to get past their own anger.

When these two important components, the love and the supporting evidence of that love, are in place, participants can share concerns. The concerns they will share with their alcoholic or chemically dependent loved ones are examples of specific symptoms of the disease. If we can talk about the symptoms of the disease rather than about bad behavior or screw-ups by the individual, then we can frame things in a way they can hear. Because the natural defense mechanisms of impaired individuals include the ability to excuse, rationalize, and justify events surrounding their disease, this particular piece of the intervention preparation is designed to neutralize and get past those defense mechanisms.

It is important to share with impaired individuals the facts of their impairment and their specific symptoms:

What happened?
When did it happen?
How did the situation affect you and the rest of the family system?

To help understand the preparation for this part of the intervention process, let's go back to the young man we cited previously. This young adult was a junior in high school and had been excelling in basketball. In his junior year, however, he realized he was only playing basketball in the hope of solidifying his relationship with his father and that it really was not fun for him anymore. At the beginning of his junior year he decided not to go out for basketball. Here is how he shared his recollection of that event and how he portrayed his father's symptoms of alcoholism:

> Dad, as much as I care, I am equally concerned. Do you remember last fall when I told you I did not want to go out for basketball? You became very angry and quickly began calling me all sorts of names, including being a quitter, a sissy, a wimp, and many other names that are too painful to mention. Not only did your angry words get out of control but you began throwing me around and hitting me. You had been drinking that night. How much I don't know, but enough that your speech was slurred and, fortunately, your coordination was very poor. Dad, I don't believe for a moment that what occurred that night would have occurred if it had not been for alcohol and your alcohol problem. Sober, you would never act that way or ever intentionally try to physically harm me.

Notice what was shared: It is nonjudgmental. It is caring but points out the symptoms of the disease: their effects upon the alcoholic, and their effects upon his son.

Not only is an intervention being done on the alcoholic, but also on the dysfunctional family system and on the secrets of that system. The son in this case has progressed, as a result of the preparation, to a point where he is able to view what is happening as symptomatic of the disease and to objectively view those symptoms and their impact on him and his father.

An important piece of this young man's statement was the last sentence: "Dad, I know this wouldn't have happened if you hadn't been drinking." What this sentence says is, "I love you and I care about you. Apart from the disease, you are okay. It is the disease I am confronting and it is you who I am loving and supporting."

Each member of the family who witnessed the event described by the seventeen-year-old was affected by the surfacing of the symptoms of the disease, but each was affected differently from the young man. The effects upon a small child are far different from the effects on a seventeen-year-old. In interventions some family members often don't want to talk about the same event because someone else already has. But what is important about the event is each individual's perception of it and its impact on him or her.

Let's take the same situation in the same family and view it through the eyes of the spouse. She verbalized her concerns about that evening this way:

> Honey, Brad has shared with you about the night when he told you he wanted to quit basketball. I would like to share with you some things you don't know about that night that occurred only because of the drinking. After you were done fighting with Brad, you left and squealed the tires of the car on the way out. I did not see you again until early morning. Brad also left and I did not hear from him for several hours.

The fear that I lived with until I heard from Brad was immense. I did not know whether or not he was okay, whether he was so hurt he would do harm to himself, or whether he had been in an accident.

He finally called me four hours later. He was okay and at a friend's. I felt a tremendous sense of relief just knowing he was okay, but I had no idea about your safety. Did you get in a car accident? Did you get arrested for drunk driving? If you did get in an accident, were you hurt? Was someone else hurt?

I could see the fear in our daughter's face [the daughter is eight years old]. I paced the floor. I worried. I tried to act brave and tried to pretend that everything was fine. I know that intentionally you would not want any of that evening to have occurred or ever to have it recur. But John, when you drink your personality changes and your actions become unpredictable. You are not the problem. But alcohol is a problem.

Take special notice again of the fact that this statement includes the components necessary for a successful intervention. It is loving. It is gentle. It is specific in the way it demonstrates the symptoms of the disease of alcoholism. And most of all, it points out that alcohol, not the individual, is the villain.

Keep uppermost in your mind that the goal of careful preparation is to neutralize the belief system of the alcoholic and bypass the defense mechanisms this disease creates, so that recovery can begin. Since this is such a critical aspect, let's review the belief system we are trying to neutralize and the defense mechanisms we are trying to bypass. The belief system of:

1. I know I have a problem, but . . .
2. Nobody would understand.
3. Nobody would accept me.
4. I am different, I am unique.
5. I'm stuck—what's the use.

It is this belief system that triggers the defense mechanisms of denial. These dominant defense mechanisms surface:

1. Rationalization
2. Justification
3. Minimization
4. Blaming
5. Excusing
6. Making alibis
7. Anger

The participants' statements above neutralize the belief system and bypass the defense mechanisms. The manner and style in which they are written and presented express understanding and caring. Anger will bring an angry response. Blaming will bring blaming. Excusing or justifying will bring excusing or justifying. The statements cited have none of these problems.

As the preparation and rehearsal process continues, each participant's script for the intervention is carefully checked by the trained interventionist in order to eliminate words or phrases that might hook the alcoholic's defense mechanisms in a way that would be destructive to the intervention process. Words and phrases like "I think," "kind of," "sort of," "maybe"—all of these tend to rescue and enable the individual.

Once everyone's data sheet has been reviewed by the interventionist, the participants are ready for the rehearsal.

The Rehearsal

The goal of rehearsing the intervention is twofold:

> To help family and friends feel the power they have collectively
>
> To help participants get an idea of how the alcoholic will respond and to help them grasp the potential for success

The interventionist will have given considerable thought to the seating arrangements for the intervention. He or she will have thought out carefully who will be sitting next to the alcoholic and in what order people will be presenting their data. Also, the interventionist may have somebody sit in the alcoholic's chair to enhance the realness of the rehearsal. The interventionist will be watching for difficulties to surface that would disrupt the intervention process. He or she will be observing whose anger is getting hooked, who wants to start ad-libbing. He or she will be watching for the fear level that exists among the participants and providing whatever reassurance is necessary to help make participation in the actual intervention possible. If one of the participants does begin getting into his or her anger, it simply means that more work with that individual is needed. I define anger as stuffed hurt and stuffed fear.

By continuing to work with those individuals who are angry, we will be able to get past that anger and help them communicate the hurt and fear they are feeling.

After the rehearsal has been completed, participants are asked to share their opinions on how successful they perceive the process to be. If this rehearsal had been the actual intervention, what would the chances have been that the individual would have entered treatment? Ten percent? Fifty percent? Ninety percent? In other words, what is the level of optimism among the participants? Typically what happens is that a group of individuals who used to feel hopeless will now feel empowered; they will be extremely optimistic that they can make a difference and that they are going to be successful in reaching the one they care about.

Once the group of significant others feels this sense of empowerment, they are ready to face the question of where to do the intervention and how to get the chemically dependent person to the intervention. It is not advisable to do the intervention on the alcoholic's turf, whether that is in his or her home or office. Whenever possible, the intervention should be done in the interventionist's office. In the history of intervention, the alcoholic was often lied to to get him or her to the meeting, or people simply walked in and surprised him or her. It is best to avoid that. It hooks the defense mechanisms and gives the chemically dependent person an opportunity to make excuses and rationalize the whole thing because he or she was lied to.

Whenever a family member comes to me to initiate the intervention process, after the first session I ask that individual to share with his or her loved one that he or she has seen a therapist and is going to continue to do so, and that at some point in time others are going to be asked to come along. The only time I do not do it that way is when there is a threat of violence or the risk of such a statement causing the loved one to run. This announcement needs to be shared with the alcoholic when he or she is sober, not when he or she has been drinking. It is not something to be debated or argued about, but simply a statement of fact to be made.

If the alcoholic get defensive when he or she is told that a loved one is seeking help, that individual has been instructed to say that he or she was asked not to argue about it or discuss it, but simply to inform. This accomplishes a couple of positive things. First, the family member no longer feels the need to sneak out to meetings with the interventionist. And second, it gives the chemically dependent person an opportunity to think about his or her disease. Secretly he or she knows that the concern is about the alcoholism and that at some point in time he or she is going to have to face it.

This announcement will often bring about a change in the drinking pattern and subsequent behavior, providing an opportunity for the family to prepare for intervention in a less tense manner. Don't let that temporary change, however, delude you into believing that things are better now. Remember that we are dealing with a disease that is progressive and has a very predictable and definable course. An interruption of that course is only temporary, and you can trust the disease to resurface and continue its downward spiral.

The alcoholic is not necessarily told that the meeting he or she has been asked to attend is about him or her and his or her alcoholism, but the alcoholic at least knows that he or she is coming to see a therapist. Because part of the alcoholic's belief system is that he or she knows alcohol is a problem for him or her, the alcoholic fully expects the problem to be raised. If, after careful consideration, the consensus of the group participating in the intervention is that the individual who started this process is not the best person to get the alcoholic to the intervention, then other strategies are developed.

Once the participants are confident that they can succeed with the intervention and that the individual asked to bring the chemically dependent person to the intervention will be successful, they are ready to schedule and proceed with the intervention. If the intervention is scheduled for 9:00 A.M., all of the participants except the one bringing the alcoholic are asked to be there at 8:30 A.M. Having all of the participants come early allows them to bring up any concerns that may have arisen since the rehearsal and allows the interventionist to reassure the participants that they are doing the right thing. The participants are asked to park their vehicles out of the alcoholic's view to prevent difficulties from arising before the actual intervention begins.

An Intervention

To understand how the intervention itself proceeds, it helps to look at an example in detail. We return then to Brad, the seventeen-year-old we have already met, and his alcoholic father, John. Here is the intervention that was prepared by Brad's father's family and friends.

Present for this intervention is a man by the name of Scott who coached Little League with John several years ago. They were very close friends at the time but have had very little contact lately. Also present are the people who live across the street, Bryan and Martha, who have been neighbors for twenty years, as well as Brad and his eight-year-old sister, Jennifer. The spouse, Karen, will be bringing John, the alcoholic, at 9:00 A.M. Scott will be sitting next to John; Bryan will be sitting on the other side of John, with Martha seated next to Bryan. Jennifer will sit next to the interventionist on one side, and Karen will sit on the other side with Brad seated next to her. The first few minutes are devoted to answering last-minute questions, to reviewing how the intervention is going to begin and proceed, and to providing reassurance, especially for the children.

At about 8:50 A.M. the interventionist asks the group to remain quiet so the alcoholic does not hear several voices and get frightened away before the process begins. The interventionist leaves the office, closes the door, and waits in the waiting room to greet the alcoholic immediately upon his entrance. The plan devised to get the alcoholic to come to the intervention session has been a success; the spouse and the alcoholic arrive promptly at 9:00 A.M.

The spouse introduces the interventionist to the alcoholic and they both shake hands with the interventionist, who takes a deep breath through his nose to see if he can smell any alcohol. It is extremely important that the intervention take place at a time when the alcoholic has not been drinking or taking drugs. If the interventionist smells alcohol, he or she will likely say, "John, we need to reschedule our visit because one of the requirements I have is that people not be drinking when I meet with them. So let's reschedule and find another time." Though this rescheduling may be difficult for the participants, it is nevertheless essential. If the individual has been drinking, the defense mechanisms will be so pronounced that the chances of success will be extremely small.

Since in this instance the individual has not been drinking, the interventionist guides the alcoholic and his spouse to the intervention room, where the intervention team is waiting. When the alcoholic walks into the room he is immediately shown to his chair. He is in a bit of a state of shock at seeing people he had not expected to see here and asks rather loudly, "What in the hell is going on here?" His friend Scott says, "John, please sit down." And the interventionist takes over.

The interventionist begins by explaining to the alcoholic what is happening:

INTERVENTIONIST: John, your family and your friends have been working with me for some time to find a way of accomplishing two very important goals. The first goal is to be able to share with you how much they care about you. And second, they want to be able to share how concerned they are. Everybody here has done a lot of hard work to prepare for this meeting today.

As a part of that preparation, I have asked everybody here to agree to some ground rules that I have for this type of a meeting. I want to ask you to agree to the same rules. John, everybody here has agreed not to interrupt while you are talking, and before we begin I am asking you to agree not to interrupt them. Can you do that, John?

(John reluctantly nods his head.)

John, am I to assume by the nod of your head that you have agreed not to interrupt people here just as they have agreed not to interrupt you?

(John quietly says yes.)

The only other rule I have, John, for this type of a meeting is that it is time-limited. This meeting will not go beyond an hour and a half. Everybody here has agreed to give up that amount of time to be with you and participate in this meeting. And before we begin I would ask that you agree to be here for that amount of time also.

(John grudgingly agrees to the time rule. Once John has agreed to the ground rules, the interventionist reviews with him how the meeting will progress and what they hope to accomplish.)

John, as I shared with you earlier, everyone here has worked hard at preparing for this meeting with the hope of being able to communicate to you their love for you and their concern—concern about what they see alcohol doing to you. John, I will be calling on each person here one at a time. They will be sharing with you what they have carefully prepared and when they are all done you and I will have a chance to talk.

(John squirms in his chair, but because what is occurring is being communicated in a gentle and nonthreatening way, John does not verbalize his discomfort. The interventionist calls on Scott. Remember that Scott is an old coaching friend with whom John has spent very little time in the last several years.)

Scott, what would you like to share with your friend John?

(Scott begins by holding his script in his hand and reading it slowly and carefully so as not to make any mistakes. He makes a lot of eye contact with John.)

SCOTT: John, I am here today to be a support to you and a support to your family. I consider you to be one of the finer people I know. I recall our days together in Little League and how much I admired your talent, not only in working with kids and bringing out the best in them, but your ability to handle the disgruntled parents who felt their children had not played enough. You were able to deal with those situations without any anger, without ever belittling the parents involved. You always took time for them, you listened, and you showed that you cared about their child. Not only was it a pleasure to work with you, but it was a real pleasure to learn from you. You had a special talent in working with people, and above all you were a marvelous role model for the kids we were coaching.

You are a good person, John, and I care about you a great deal. And it is because I care that I also want to tell you that I am concerned. I am concerned about what I see happening to you and your family. I know very little firsthand about your drinking because, for whatever reasons, you choose not to accept our invitations to dinner or for get-togethers. You have slowly withdrawn from our friendship. Even though I have not witnessed your drinking problem firsthand, I want you to know that I trust the perceptions of everybody else in this room. And because I care about you as they do, I share their pain and their hurt for you and for them. I want you to hear this group of people out.

Hear the love they have for you, the concern they have, and then accept the help that will be offered to you.

(Scott is now finished. The interventionist moves immediately to the next participant, Bryan, to allow no time for the defenses of the alcoholic to begin surfacing.)

INTERVENTIONIST: Bryan, what would you like to share with John?

BRYAN: John, I am here today because I care about you. We have been neighbors for nearly twenty years. We have socialized together. Our children have grown up together. We have supported each other through the difficult times of being parents as well as having shared many of the joys. For several years I have wanted to be able to reach out to you and say something about your drinking. But I haven't known how.

John, about six months ago at 10:30 at night, Karen came over [Karen is John's spouse] and asked if I could come over and help you. Brad wasn't home and you were passed out in the car in the driveway and she needed some help to get you in the house. I know you don't remember it, but I do. As you partially came to, you began crying at the embarrassment of having me see you like that. We got you upstairs to bed, got your shoes off, and let you sleep it off. I came back home without saying much to Karen.

Martha and I talked that night about how painful it must be for your wife and your children. And how painful it must be for you. I know how much you love your family and how much they love you. Sometimes at night when you come home late and intoxicated and you and Karen get in a fight, we can hear the shouting and screaming inside our house. I have wanted to come over but I don't want to interfere. And John, I am the one who called the police a few weeks ago. Things sounded so out of control that I was scared for the safety of your family. John, I know lately you have talked about leaving the family. I don't believe for a moment that that is what you want, because the only time I hear you talking that way is after you have been drinking.

Being involved in preparing for this intervention, John, I have learned about the disease of alcoholism and how much pain it causes the family, but also how much pain it causes the alcoholic. I know you must hurt very badly inside about what has been happening to you and your family. I am asking you today to stop that hurt and that pain and to accept the treatment that will be offered to you.

(The interventionist moves the process forward and next calls on the seventeen-year-old son, Brad.)

BRAD: I'm here because I love you. Dad, there have been times when I have felt especially close to you. I don't know whether it was because I am your oldest son, but there are many times when I have felt like my relationship with you has been special.

I remember feeling so proud when you coached my baseball team. I remember the pine-box derby, which was a father-and-son project, and even though the car we made didn't have a chance at winning, and might even have been a little ugly, we did it together. And you really made me feel included and special.

Dad, as much as I care, I am equally concerned. Do you remember last fall when I told you I did not want to go out for basketball? You became very angry and quickly began calling me all sorts of names, including being a quitter, a sissy, a wimp, and many other names that are too painful to mention. Not only did your angry words get out of control but you began throwing me around and hitting me. You had been drinking that night. How much I don't know, but enough that your speech was slurred and, fortunately, your coordination was very poor. Dad, I don't believe for a moment that what occurred that night would have occurred if it had not been for alcohol and your alcohol problem. Sober, you would never act that way or ever intentionally try to physically harm me.

(In addition to the above incident Brad also talks about how he feels about the way his dad treats his mom when his dad drinks. He ends his sharing with the following.)

Dad in less than a year I am going off to college. If you can accept help today we have a chance to restore our relationship before it is too late. There is still time for us to get back to being the friends we once were, but that time is short. And I don't want to waste it. Dad, please go to treatment before it is too late for us.

(Martha, the neighbor, speaks next.)

MARTHA: John, I am also here because I love you. You have been a very special friend, and you and your wife have been special confidants over the years. Rather than speak about the times when your alcohol problem has affected and hurt me, I would like to share with you what has happened in our house as a result of this same problem.

As you know, John, our son, Bryan Jr., has had a problem with drugs. We had to place him in treatment. What I want to share with you are the results, and what has happened to our family as a result of his recovery. We all participated in Bryan's treatment, and as a result our family is closer today and happier today than probably it has ever been. Yes, there was a lot of heartache and a lot of pain that we had to walk through, but both he and our entire family are on the road to recovery.

I want so much for you and your family to be able to experience the other side of this problem. John, for you, your own sake, and for your family, will you please go to treatment today?

(The spouse goes next.)

KAREN: John, I am here today because I love you. Over the years you have been my rock. And more than my husband, you have been my friend. John, everything we have worked so hard to build is slowly being destroyed by alcohol and the control it has over you.

(She shares her view of the basketball incident. As she proceeds she begins to dispel the myth that the alcoholic feels that nobody knows and nobody would understand.)

John, I have tried every way I know how to help, except the right way. I've tried to cover up. I've tried

84

to protect you. I've tried to defend you. I've lied to our friends and our neighbors and my parents about what was happening. In spite of those efforts, everybody knows that you've got a problem. My parents know. Your mother knows. Our friends, our neighbors, the school, they all know that John has a drinking problem.

Today I am choosing to stop pretending that alcohol is not a problem. I am going to get the help I need and I am going to get the kids the help they need so that we can begin healing. John, I want you to get treatment, too. If you don't, our kids are not going to want to come home from college. They will not want to bring their fiancées home. They won't want you at their weddings. And they won't want to bring our grandchildren to visit.

I dread the thought of that occurring, but I know that without treatment all of those things are possible. John, please enter treatment today for you and for us so that we can have the kind of marriage that we have had in the past, and we can be a family again.

(Jennifer, the eight-year-old daughter and the apple of her dad's eye, speaks next. She is trying hard to hold back her tears and for a moment cries openly. The interventionist gives her some support, lets her cry for a moment, helps her take a couple of slow, deep breaths, and says, "Jennifer, can you share what you have written to your daddy?")

JENNIFER: (In a trembling and tearful voice) Daddy, I love you. Daddy, for my eighth birthday party I asked Mommy if I could have it after school while you were at work so I wouldn't be embarrassed in front of my friends by your drinking. Daddy, I am afraid if you don't go to treatment you're going to leave our family and I don't want us to not be a family anymore. Daddy, please go to treatment.

(Jennifer is now sobbing openly. The interventionist allows Jennifer to continue sobbing and over the tears begins speaking to John. John's eyes have also moistened.)

INTERVENTIONIST: John, your family and your friends have taken a significant risk today. They have taken the risk of sharing with you their love for you, and their concern about what they see alcohol doing to you, in the hope of being able to reach you and give you the support and the courage you need to take that first step of accepting treatment. I know it has to have been very hard for you to sit here, not to interrupt, and to hear the pain that is in your loved ones' hearts.

Let me explain to you the kind of treatment they are asking you to receive and what it is about. John, your family is asking you to go to an inpatient treatment facility where you can learn about the disease that you have and what it is you need to do to take care of it. They have visited a number of treatment facilities, and the one they believe will work best for you and for them is Cottonwood Treatment Center.

(The interventionist explains to John some of what occurs in treatment and answers his questions about the treatment process.)

John, I am sure you are concerned about work and a number of other issues. I want to share with you that your family has arranged with your employer for you to take whatever time off from work is necessary until you are released from the treatment center. And your medical insurance will cover the full cost of treatment. Every possible obstacle your family and friends were able to anticipate that might stand in the way of your beginning treatment today has been dealt with and taken care of. If, for whatever reasons, there are some they have forgotten, we will go to work on eliminating those obstacles so that you can accept the help you need.

(John begins to speak. He first verbalizes his anger about his employer knowing his situation. Then he starts to apologize to his family and friends for the embarrassment he has caused them and the embarrassment he is now feeling. At an opportune moment the interventionist interjects.)

John, your family understands that the acts that have occurred were not willful acts. They were symptoms of the disease of alcoholism. What your family needs to hear today, far more than apologies, is action. John, will you go with your family and friends and enter treatment?

(Over the next five minutes, which to the family feel like an hour, the interventionist interacts with the alcoholic, helping to move him slowly to the point of surrender. On two or three different occasions during that time, the interventionist repeats the same question.)

John, will you enter treatment today?

(The interventionist is careful to make sure that John fully comprehends what it is that his family is asking him to

do. They are asking him to enter an inpatient treatment facility. They are asking him to stay for the duration of that treatment—twenty-eight to thirty-five days. And they are asking him to do it now, not this afternoon or tomorrow or next week, but now. The interventionist reviews this with the alcoholic a couple of times to make sure there is no misunderstanding. He then again repeats his question.)

John, are you willing to enter treatment? Will you do it?

(Slowly, John nods his head. But the interventionist wants more than a nod.)

John, am I to assume by the nod of your head that you are agreeing to enter treatment? Can you say yes?

(John says yes. The family embraces him, congratulates him, and soon they are on their way to treatment.)

The intervention that has just been described to you is not at all atypical. The time that has elapsed from when the intervention began at 9:00 A.M. to when the patient agreed to enter treatment is only about twenty minutes. Though an hour and a half was planned, the intervention is often over and the alcoholic is on his way to treatment long before that time has expired. All of the family members and friends who participated in the intervention go with the alcoholic to get him checked into treatment. They may already have a bag packed for him. If not, they will bring his clothes to the treatment center later that day.

At check-in time at the treatment facility, the family signs up for the family program and makes their own commitment to recovery. If the intervention has been especially difficult, the interventionist may schedule a debriefing session for later that day or the following day.

Contrast and compare this typical intervention with the original concept of intervention described on pages 30 to 34. Notice the absence of confrontation and the absence of anger, defensiveness, and blame on the part of the alcoholic. The absence of confrontation allowed the intervention process to get past the defense mechanisms of the alcoholic, neutralize his belief system, and move the individual forward into treatment.

The confrontational style hooked the alcoholic's defense mechanisms; it caused him to shout, to express extreme anger, and as discussed by Vernon Johnson in *I'll Quit Tomorrow*, to "go nose-to-nose with his daughter until he had reduced her to tears." If the intervention process is truly intervention rather than confrontation, all of that can be prevented. If anger does surface during intervention, it will be at a far more manageable level and can be readily handled by a trained interventionist.

Because we are dealing with a disease that is chronic and progressive, the sooner you intervene the better. The sooner you intervene, the easier it will be for the alcoholic to accept treatment, and the less defensive he or she will become. And the sooner you intervene, the better the prognosis is for recovery.

5

Frequently Asked Questions

In the more than one thousand interventions I have done, the fears expressed and questions asked by significant others frequently have been the same:

1. **"Why is it important to have the children present during the intervention?"**

   The spouse of the alcoholic is often concerned about involving the children. Family members of an alcoholic, particularly the children, often feel that they are doing something to cause the problem. Getting them involved educates them about the disease of alcoholism and helps to bring them a sense of emotional freedom. They need to learn that what is occurring is a disease and that they do not cause diseases.

   The children, whatever their ages, have been living with a lot of repressed and pent-up feelings.

They need an opportunity to express their feelings and deal with the traumatic effects of this disease. The intervention process does not expose them to anything they do not already know about. And by being able to participate, they can learn the facts rather than be burdened with what their young minds have imagined. What they imagine is always much worse than what is. In addition, unless they have been physically or sexually abused, children have the capacity to be emotionally honest, and the younger they are the freer they are to share what is in their hearts. If they are old enough to absorb and share the pain and the trauma that this disease causes, they are old enough to share the joy of the beginning stages of recovery. If one of the children has been the family scapegoat, the interventionist will keep boundaries in place to prevent scapegoating from occurring during the intervention process.

In the old style of intervention, the power came from confrontation. In this style of intervention the power comes from love. Children are able to communicate love in their own childlike but powerful way.

I remember an intervention a number of years ago in which a five-year-old daughter participated. I allow small children to be their natural selves and to write their own scripts. In this situation Mom and Dad were separated and Mom had told her daughter that the reason they were separated was because Dad had a drinking problem and would not get help. When the daughter visited Dad she told him what Mom had said. Dad's response was, "Well, I would get some help but I'm too broke."

The daughter came to the intervention, which happened to occur on Valentine's Day. She had placed in an envelope several little candy hearts that said "I Love You," plus twenty-six cents of her savings. She walked over and gave her father the envelope and said, with tears in her eyes, "Daddy, I love you. And I know you said you could not get help because you were broke, so here is some money for you." I know of nothing more meaningful than the simple love of a child. That little girl's father not only got well but changed careers and is now a professional in the field of alcohol treatment.

With guidance, children are not only capable of handling the intervention process but are far better off emotionally for being involved in it. And if intervention fails, for whatever reasons, the education they have received will help them understand that what is going on with their parent is not their fault, and they will know that they have tried to help. If they have not participated and the intervention fails, they will second-guess themselves and wish that they had been there. They may also believe that it is their fault that the intervention didn't work.

2. **"Why can't we have just family? Won't he or she be embarrassed by having friends here?"**
The answer to the latter question is yes, because the alcoholic already secretly feels embarrassed; the intervention simply makes the embarrassment public. The goal of intervention, however, is not to embarrass the alcoholic but to help the alcoholic accept help. To succeed in doing this one needs to ap-

proach intervention differently from the manner in which every other crisis that has resulted from his or her disease has been approached. It has been a dysfunctional approach to try to keep the alcoholism a secret.

Several years ago I had the opportunity to hear a speaker, whose name I do not recall, on dysfunctional family systems. One of the things she stated was this: If you can figure out what the rules of the dysfunctional family system are, the healthiest thing you can do for that family is to begin breaking the rules.

One of the primary rules of the alcoholic family is secrecy. If we are going to be successful, we must break the secret. The reality is that alcoholism is not a secret at all. Family and friends know that your loved one is impaired. They may not know the depth and breadth of it, and they may not know specific details of what has been going on, but they know there is a problem. And you will find that friends have been waiting for you to say something.

The involvement of people outside the family is important for a number of reasons:

1. It breaks the family secret.
2. There is safety and strength in numbers.
3. The alcoholic does not want to embarrass himself or herself in front of people outside the family.
4. Their presence prevents the alcoholic from blaming the spouse or the children.
5. They provide much-needed support for the family.

3. "Will I have to talk about _____?"

   The alcoholic's spouse is frequently concerned about the washing of some very private linen in public, such as impotence or an affair that the alcoholic or the spouse has had. The spouse may not want to discuss such things in front of children or friends. Remember that the goal of intervention is not to embarrass or to shame the alcoholic into treatment, but to bathe him or her in love and reality.

   Private and painful matters often do not need to be brought out in the intervention. It is extremely important, however, that you have a private session with the interventionist to discuss these things. The more the interventionist knows about the difficulties the alcoholic is experiencing, no matter how painful they may be, the more the interventionist can help you structure and plan the intervention to be a success. The interventionist is only as good as the data provided and cannot control or structure the intervention in a way that will be successful if you keep secrets from him or her. Rest assured that this information will be kept private.

   Remember that guilt and shame are powerful deterrents to the acceptance of treatment. If the interventionist knows about those critical issues, the intervention can be structured to bypass them. When these sensitive issues are part of the disease, and when as interventionist I see that the alcoholic is refusing treatment but is unable to verbalize any concrete reason for it, I ask the family and friends to give me a few moments alone with the alcoholic and the spouse. In that private time I let the alcoholic know that I know what's been happening and that it's okay and not uncommon with alcoholism, and I say that in treatment he or she will be relieved of the guilt and the shame. When the alcoholic understands that what has occurred is all right, and that help is available, and that he or she won't be shamed for what has happened, a very difficult obstacle has been overcome. It is therefore critically important, even though there may be items you do not want brought out in the intervention, to make those things known to the interventionist so he or she can structure and plan the intervention accordingly.

4. "But what if it doesn't work?"

Nothing works 100 percent of the time. You need to keep in mind that we are dealing with a disease that causes irrational responses. Thus it is impossible to predict the outcome of intervention with absolute certainty. If, however, your intervention is properly prepared and you have the assistance of a trained professional, the chances of it being successful are over 90 percent, with success defined as having your loved one enter treatment.

But what if it fails? If it fails and the alcoholic refuses to accept treatment of any kind, the worst that can happen is that you will know you have tried. You will know that you have walked the extra mile and have done all that you can do. You will no longer have to pretend. You will no longer have to keep a family secret, and you will become emotionally free to make healthy decisions to take good care of yourself and your children. Because your loved one has a disease that has an identifiable course of deterioration, it will provide ample opportunities for intervention at a later date or will create natural crises that will provide opportunities for the alcoholic to get a grasp on reality at another time.

Dick Selvig, who spent thirty-plus years working in the field of addictions, taught me an important lesson. He said that I, as a professional, am responsible only for the message that I give and how I give it, not whether or not it is acted upon. By intervening you give a powerful message of love and hope to the alcoholic. Do not assume responsibility for whether or not it is heard. Remember that even though the alcoholic may have heard the message, he or she may not be able to act on it on the exact timetable you might wish. But the possibility of acting on the message of love and hope may still occur at a later date.

I know of no one who has participated in a failed intervention who did not feel a tremendous sense of relief at having gone through the process, in spite of the failure. Even though they were unsuccessful, they were immediately grateful for having had the opportunity to try. You, your family, and the alcoholic are all worth the effort to begin recovery, whether or not that effort culminates in total success.

5. "What if I cry?"

You are dealing with subject matter that is often extremely painful, and crying is a normal, natural, and healthy response to pain. Tears during the intervention process are not counterproductive; rather, they tell the alcoholic nonverbally that you care. If you didn't care, it wouldn't hurt so much. Sharing your pain gives the alcoholic permission to begin facing his or her pain.

The family disease of addiction forces one to repress pain. Because the recovery process begins the first time you see the interventionist, it is okay to start doing things differently, to stop the repression and begin letting the pain out.

6. **"How many persons should be involved?"**
There is no absolute number. Six to eight persons is average, but who is involved is more important than how many are involved. Those close to the individual—his or her family, such as parents, spouse, children, and in-laws—should be involved if at all possible. It is equally important that people outside the family—neighbors, friends, and others whom the alcoholic respects—be involved also. Successful interventions have been done with as few as one person participating and as many as fifteen. The ideal, however, is six to eight.

The person beginning the intervention initially may find it difficult to think of others who might be willing to be involved. The only way to find out is to ask. Remember that you are asking them simply to meet with the interventionist to explore possibilities, not to make a commitment to participate in the intervention. Then they will be able to decide on their own whether or not to be involved, based upon some knowledge of what will be occurring. Most people will respect your wish that they at least come and listen.

7. **"Why do I feel disloyal, as if I were sneaking around behind the person's back?"**

Although this question may not always be verbalized, the feeling is universal. You are feeling disloyal because members of an alcoholic family feel the need to try to keep alcoholism a family secret. The rule of not talking outside the family is often multigenerational. Remember as a child how little permission there was to talk about what was happening in your family outside the home. Not only is the family rule of secrecy strong, so is your sense of guilt and shame. Somehow you believe you ought to have been able to handle this, control it, and fix it on your own without outside help.

The alcoholic, in a remorseful moment, may have elicited from you a promise not to tell the kids, his or her parents, or your parents about what occurred. Out of loyalty, you may have committed to that promise. You are feeling disloyal for a number of reasons:

1. You are being disloyal to the dysfunctional family rules.
2. You are being disloyal to promises elicited from you through remorse.
3. Your own sense of self-failing is coming to the surface and you are "shoulding" yourself to death. "I should have done this. I should have done that. I should have said this. I should have said that."

Spouses and family members of alcoholics hold lifetime memberships in the "should have" club. Don't deny those feelings of disloyalty, but don't expect them to go away. Tell them to your interventionist, keep talking about them, and keep walking through the intervention process. If you grew up in a dysfunctional family, those feelings may be especially powerful. The more you can verbalize them, the less power they will have.

8. **"How will we get the alcoholic here? What if he or she won't come?"**
Tell the one you are concerned about that you are seeking help. Beyond that, one should defer dealing with this question until all of the preparation has been done and the rehearsal has been completed. The question is far too scary to deal with at the outset and may inhibit you from following through with the intervention.

If you can wait until the preparation and the rehearsal have been completed, you will have more objectivity and clarity. The clarity, objectivity, and sense of empowerment you feel as part of the intervention team will in turn reveal numerous options that can allow this last step to be successful. A trained interventionist can share options with you and the others involved in the intervention and can assess the likelihood of their success.

9. **"Is it normal to feel like it won't work? Is it normal to feel like it will fail?"**
Yes. Remember that you have tried many times in many ways to get your loved one to face his or her alcoholism. It is difficult to believe that this attempt can elicit any response different from before. If you follow through with the preparation process and heed

the guidance of your interventionist, that feeling will slowly dissipate and be replaced with feelings of hope and optimism.

10. "Will this make the alcoholic violent?"
Unless there has been a history of violence, the chance of it occurring as a result of the intervention is remote. If there has been such a history, then your interventionist will work with you to provide safety for you and the others involved. A trained interventionist has dealt with this situation before and can advise you on what steps to take before the intervention is completed. There is no reason not to proceed.

11. "Has anyone committed suicide as a result of intervention?"
In the more than one thousand interventions I have done, suicide has never occurred, not even with persons who have verbalized suicidal thoughts. The intervention itself will not cause suicide. If there has been a strong verbalization of suicidal tendencies prior to the intervention, the interventionist will include components to help protect against it. In most states, if a person is an imminent threat to himself or herself or to someone else, there are actions that can be taken, including mandatory hospitalization. A trained professional can help assess this risk. Suicide is extremely unlikely.

12. "Should I try an alternative first? Is there something less intense and dramatic that I should try?"

Your interventionist can answer this question. By the time you have a gotten to the interventionist's office you have usually exhausted other options. Your repeated attempts to reach the alcoholic on your own have met with failure. You have probably already talked with his or her physician, and the physician's advice about the risks of drinking have also met with failure.

Remember that this disease is a powerful one and that it is the disease that is in control, not the person. To neutralize that power takes strength, and that strength comes from communicating with your loved one, in a controlled setting, in a controlled manner, with an interventionist and others present. One of the ways you can sort out whether or not intervention is necessary is to ask yourself and, if possible, your loved one, the following questions:

1. If I made an appointment for an evaluation, would he or she come?
2. If he or she did come, would the recommendations of the evaluator be accepted even if those recommendations included residential treatment?

If your loved one answers yes to those two questions, then intervention is unnecessary. When you have reached the point of considering intervention, the alcoholic's response is generally not only "No!" but "Hell no!" If you are unsure what the response might be, catch the alcoholic in a sober and vulnerable moment and ask. Look for a window of opportunity when he is least affected by alcohol.

Don't ask, however, unless you are prepared to immediately follow through with scheduling an evaluation. In most instances intervention is not only viable but the most caring choice you could make. You and your family deserve success, not another failed attempt.

13. **"Do I need a professional?"**

A professionally guided intervention has by far the greatest chance of success. Interventions have been done without the aid of a professional, but they are often very traumatic for the family. There may be angry exchanges, and although the family may be successful in getting their loved one to treatment, part of the treatment process is spent repairing the damage caused by the intervention.

An intervention without a professional should not be attempted in these instances:

> The alcoholic is beyond the early to middle stages of the disease.
> There is a hint of difficulties other than alcohol.
> Drugs other than alcohol are involved, including prescription drugs, cocaine, marijuana, amphetamines, or any other illegal drugs.
> There is a family history of psychiatric illness.
> There have been threats of violence or actual violence.
> There have been threats of suicide.

A basic rule of human relationships is that the closer one is to a situation or person, the less objective one is. One of the major purposes of a professionally guided intervention is to have an objective point of view. That guidance is invaluable to the intervention process. It can minimize problems and trauma such that little time needs to be spent in treatment repairing the damage caused by the intervention.

To have a professional assist and guide your intervention elevates the problem to a level of seriousness that demands the alcoholic's attention and provides a sense of security and safety for the entire family. I have never had a family tell me they wished they had done the intervention on their own. In fact, in most cases the family has expressed the belief that had it not been for professional involvement, the intervention would not have been successful.

For an intervention to be successful, all of the following must be assessed:

> What stage the disease is at
> What defense mechanisms will surface
> What will hook those defense mechanisms
> What will be necessary to bypass the defense mechanisms
> What data and how much data will be needed to get past the denial
> What treatment will be appropriate for the level of the disease

This requires not only objectivity but a considerable amount of clinical expertise. If your loved one was suffering from any other disease, you would not place on yourself the burden of assessing the progression of that disease, the manner in which to interrupt that disease, and the development of a treatment plan for it. It is extremely unwise for you to place that burden upon yourself for the disease of alcoholism or chemical dependency. I encourage you to relieve yourself of the burden of handling this disease alone and to seek and accept professional guidance.

Other Questions and Fears

It is impossible to answer every question you may have or to address each and every fear. Verbalize all your questions to the interventionist. There is no such thing as a dumb question. The questions you ask will help you feel more secure, will build trust between you and the interventionist, and will help the interventionist get a better grasp of the situation so the intervention can be structured and planned for positive results.

The same is true for your fears. Your scary feelings are not bad; they are normal and natural. You cannot talk about them too much with your interventionist. Remember that part of the intervention is breaking the unhealthy family rules that have developed with this disease. The rules of "don't trust," "don't talk," and "don't feel" need to be broken.

6

Intervention Considerations for Different Populations

Many families have come to me over the years for intervention, and each has believed that its situation is unique. Certainly to some extent this is true, but such beliefs are to a large degree a product of the family disease of alcoholism and drug addiction. And they are not at all unlike the alcoholic's or addict's feelings of uniqueness. The diseases of alcoholism and drug addiction may affect different people, but they have identifiable symptoms and a very predictable course, regardless of the position, age, or gender of those who are afflicted.

These shared characteristics allow a trained professional to predict quite accurately the outcome of intervention. In spite of the commonality, however, sometimes there are special problems. In these cases, families have special difficulties giving themselves permission to begin the intervention process and may feel quite stuck.

It is impossible in this work to cover exhaustively each and every potential situation, but I can share with you a broad enough spectrum of typical sorts of cases to help you identify with one that may be close to yours. By finding a section in this chapter that discribes a situation similar to yours, you will feel a sense of hope and be reassured that you can make a difference.

In reading the following, I encourage you to focus on the similarities between these situations and your own rather than to search for the differences.

The Corporate Executive

Many families and individuals who have someone they love in a position of power and prestige—president or chief executive officer of a major corporation, for example—feel especially powerless. Part of that sense of powerlessness stems from the fact that they regard this individual as superhuman. They are not able to see this individual as a human being subject to the same human frailties as you and I, especially to diseases like alcoholism and drug addiction.

One of the difficulties with this type of intervention is that often we are dealing with an individual who has struggled to work his or her way up through the ranks. He or she has been a mover and a shaker and has accomplished a great deal. As a result of that hard work and personal success, families may put this individual on a pedestal and fail to acknowledge his or her humanness.

Economics are also often an issue for the family of an executive. Suppose that as a result of intervening you lose your relationship and the life-style to which you have become accustomed? If the intervention is handled with dignity, respect, and love, you will achieve the response you desire.

The corporate executive, however, poses a few unique challenges, all of which are manageable. First, the corporate executive has peers who should be involved. That may mean people in some important positions. Regardless of their personal or institutional importance, however, they respond in the same way as anyone does when he or she hears about the possibility of intervention. They have the same fears, doubts, and anxieties but, once educated, will respond with compassion and with love.

Second, corporate executives often have such busy schedules that it seems impossible to make time for the intervention. This means the intervention needs to be powerful enough that the executive feels sufficiently empowered to cancel his or her other appointments. The interventionist can help with this.

Third, we must consider the issues of confidentiality and public relations. What do we say if we are asked? What if the press finds out? A trained interventionist, working with the public relations department of the corporation, can easily and carefully devise a plan of action for dealing with these issues. Usually, it's best just to say that the individual is unavailable. Later, the patient will have recovered sufficiently to say how he or she wishes to handle the situation. Confidentiality and privacy are extremely important, especially for the executive. A trained interventionist can help deal with this issue.

Certain issues that need to be dealt with will arise with every intervention. The professional's role is to help develop a strategy to keep these issues from interfering with recovery. Some issues may require much time, energy, and money, but no issue is more important than the life of your loved one.

In all cases, the process is virtually the same:

We begin with one person.
We educate that person.
We expand our program to include others.
We educate others.
We carefully prepare and rehearse.
We eliminate the excuses.
We intervene.
And we go to treatment.

If the intervention involves an executive, you may find that the only major difference is whether you go by car or by corporate jet.

The Professional Person

By professionals I mean medical doctors, dentists, priests, ministers, lawyers, accountants, psychologists, and others of similar status. The family may place the professional on a pedestal in much the same way they would a corporate executive. This response to the professional is most unfair and inhumane. Because most professionals are licensed, often the conspiracy of silence on the part of family and friends is far stronger than it would otherwise be. Families get caught up in the fear of the loss of the professional's right to practice, and as a result they get trapped in a web of silence and subsequent enabling.

Also, I believe we as a culture have treated our professionals very unfairly and in many ways have not allowed them to be human. Consequently, the families of professionals and the professionals themselves have a difficult time acknowledging drug or alcohol addictions. As a result, often we do not intervene until the problem becomes obvious at work.

I recall an intervention I did a number of years ago on a physician. He was drinking heavily each evening and frequently having blackouts. For more than three years, when the phone rang in the evening, his spouse got on the extension and recorded the name of the caller and what medical advice or prescriptions he gave. Before he went to work in the morning, she sat down at the breakfast table and reviewed with him the medical calls of the night before.

Such an enabling conspiracy of silence is not at all uncommon among families of professionals. As a result, often we do not intervene on professionals until the disease is so far advanced that treatment is difficult and the prognosis poor. By waiting, we only increase the risk to their health, to their livelihoods, and even to their patients. I have never seen a case where it was too early to intervene, only ones where it was too late, or nearly so.

Most of the professional governing boards in this country today have groups for addicted professionals. These groups have been put together to reach those who need help before disciplinary or legal action is necessary. However, too frequently the professional group hears about the problem only after it has reached crisis level and legal action has already begun. You may anonymously call the local governing board of the professional organization to which your loved one belongs and ask what services are available.

An important factor to consider with professionals is

the involvement of peers. However, one of the big mistakes made with interventions on medical professionals is that one assumes that a doctor is educated about the disease of alcoholism. Sadly, that is not true.

Alcoholism and drug addiction are our number-one health problems. Medical schools, however, still do not deal adequately with these subjects. Therefore, I require physicians involved in interventions to go through exactly the same education as the rest of the participants. We prepare the same way, we bathe them in love the same way, and we immerse them in reality the same way. It helps to involve the patient's professional peers, but it is not necessary.

For clergy it is most important, if possible, that a spiritual superior be involved in the intervention process along with peers. For clergy who do not have families, we involve as many fellow clerics or nuns in the intervention as possible. The love and support of fellow clerics or nuns are as powerful as the love and support of spouse and children.

For the most part, people in the helping professions are there because they are dedicated to helping others. Above all, they do not want to be in a position where they may be hurting others. Because of this, intervention is quite straightforward. However, although they are dedicated to helping others, they have a difficult time giving themselves permission to accept help. Once that hurdle is crossed, they are on the road to treatment and subsequent recovery.

In addition, professionals often feel more guilt and shame than other alcoholics and addicts. That guilt and shame make it all the more important that we intervene rather than confront. Confrontation tends to reinforce guilt and shame; the patient hears "I am bad," not "I am sick."

Often because of the extent to which professional alcoholics or addicts are protected by family, office staffs, and peers, the disease tends to become more advanced than it does in the general population. Greater planning and preparation, however, can make intervention more effective.

The Housewife

The female alcoholic, in particular the housewife, often gets trapped in the disease of alcoholism and drug addiction by our cultural bias. There is a great deal of difference in our culture between "drinking like a man" and "drinking like a lady." Men with drinking problems become alcoholics. Women with drinking problems, particularly housewives, become lushes.

The belief that addiction is a male disease often impedes the intervention process when dealing with female alcoholics. Men are much quicker to divorce the female alcoholic rather than intervene. The extended family also has more difficulty coming to grips with women alcoholics— the denial is stronger, the secrecy greater.

The symptoms of alcoholism conflict with what our culture considers to be womanly or motherly. As a result the woman/housewife alcoholic is quickly forced into secrecy, and most of the symptoms of her disease occur behind closed doors. The female alcoholic really believes that "No one would understand" and "No one could possibly accept me if they knew." The guilt and the shame are enormous.

The more pronounced the alcoholic's defense mechanisms, guilt, and shame, the more pronounced the family's. Nowhere is this more true than in the family of the female alcoholic. It is a perfect example of the elephant-in-the-living-room syndrome. The special problems of the female alcoholic are not with the alcoholic herself, but with her family. It is difficult for the spouse and the children to give themselves permission to go outside the family, break the family secret, and talk about what is going on behind closed doors.

Often this intervention is started by a friend or one of the older children rather than by the spouse. Frequently the first step in this intervention process is to deal with the shame and denial of the spouse and the rest of the family and to give them the permission needed to proceed with intervention.

Perhaps the best example of the female alcoholic's extreme defense mechanisms is this: 90 percent of male alcoholics or addicts cry when they reach the decision to accept help as a result of intervention. They are able then to show at least some of their pain and other feelings. For the female alcoholic, it is the opposite: 90 percent go through intervention and agree to go to treatment without showing any emotion whatsoever. Intervention is just as successful, but the female alcoholic must overcome much more repression before she can be emotionally alive again.

Once the closeted female alcoholic understands that what has been happening every day is not bad and evil but part of the disease, recovery can begin and hope can be restored. That process begins by first helping the family with those same emotions and hurdles. When the husband and children understand her behavior as symptomatic of the disease rather than of a lack of love or mothering, the family is on the road to recovery.

The Adolescent

The rate of alcohol and drug abuse among young people is alarming. Statistics tell us that as many as 60 percent of high-school kids are involved with chemicals on at least a weekly basis. The path to addiction for many of them will be short indeed. The difficulties of intervening with adolescents were perhaps best described by Mark Twain when he said, "When I was a boy of fourteen, my father was so ignorant I could hardly stand to have the old man around, but when I got to be twenty-one I was astonished at how much he had learned in seven years."

Because of the maturational process and the struggle for independence, often parents have very little influence over the fifteen- or sixteen-year-old. Instead, influence over adolescents comes from peers, particularly old friends whom the young addict no longer sees very often.

One of the things that routinely happens with young addicts or alcoholics is that they gravitate to a peer group that uses drugs or alcohol as much as, or more than, they do. They leave old friends behind. Those lifelong friends who have been abandoned need to be involved in the intervention process because they have a significant amount of positive influence. Also, there are other adults the young person respects: a coach, a favorite teacher, a youth pastor, a grandparent, aunt, or uncle.

It is never too soon to intervene with the adolescent. Because the adolescent is still developing physically and psychologically it is imperative that the disease be interrupted at the earliest possible stage.

Here are some signs and symptoms of alcohol and drug problems you can watch for in young people:

1. Alcohol missing from your liquor cabinet
2. Alcohol in the liquor cabinet diluted
3. A change in peer group
4. More callers who don't leave their last names
5. Calls from kids you have never heard of before
6. A drop in grades, particularly in math and science
7. Sneaking out at night
8. Selling of cassettes, records, or CDs
9. Items missing from the house
10. More secrecy
11. His or her room suddenly becoming off-limits
12. Hacking or coughing in the shower
13. Reddened eyes
14. Blank look
15. Erratic behavior
16. Unexplained emotional outbursts
17. Unauthorized absences from school
18. Pattern of tardiness at school

Most school counselors today have a good understanding of chemical dependency in adolescents and will be cooperative if you call them to share your concerns. Generally, someone at school has spotted the problem and will be able to work with you toward successfully helping the young person.

Adolescents involved in alcohol and drug-use may experiment with and/or become addicted to a variety of drugs. One needs to watch carefully for the signs and symptoms of the use of methamphetamines, cocaine, and hallucinogens such as LSD and PCP. Hallucinogenic mushrooms are also quite common in some parts of the country.

Actual addiction does not need to be present to seek

help—intervention can also be preventative. Because growth and development are still occurring in adolescents, intervention and/or consultation early on is imperative. Interrupting the drug use early, before the adolescent has become enmeshed in the drug culture is extremely important.

Successful intervention can be done on the adolescent without the parent having to kick or lock the adolescent out of the house, a strategy frequently suggested by tough-love groups. Chemical dependency can progress very rapidly in young people, and the more it progresses, the greater sense of unrealistic power the adolescent feels. As a result of that power, it is not uncommon for parents and siblings to be living in fear of their family member. That is why you cannot seek help too early when an adolescent is involved.

The Professional Woman

The professional woman may believe that she has climbed the ladder of corporate or professional success by playing by men's rules in a man's world. As a result, she often tries to drink like a man. Unfortunately, alcoholism progresses at a more rapid rate in women, and what seems to be a hallmark of their success can become the cause of their downfall.

It is very difficult for the woman professional to give herself permission to seek help on her own. She fears that there will be five men standing in the background saying, "I told you so," and fighting to move into her position. Unfortunately, her fears are somewhat justified. That is why it is extremely important to intervene with the professional woman before it affects her job. Once her disease and its symptoms show up on the job, it is difficult indeed to marshal the support from the workplace necessary to help her take the first step into treatment.

The intervention process on the professional woman needs to deal with these fears and to provide whatever safety is necessary. In addition to family and friends, it is especially helpful if a true equal of hers, one who has struggled with the same problems, can be involved in the intervention process. That person can help allay those fears even though she may not know much about the particular case. The message that her presence gives is "I survived professionally by surviving alcoholism," rather than "I survived by denying alcoholism."

The Senior Citizen

When working with the elderly, it is of paramount importance to avoid a confrontational style. Elderly alcoholics often have been alcoholics for a long time. As a result, their adult children are often filled with anger and even rage, especially if they see the problem reoccurring in the third generation. If confrontation begins, where does it stop? An onslaught of information about the disease may actually trigger a total psychological collapse. If psychological collapse does not result from a harsh confrontation with the elderly alcoholic, certainly a rupture in the family fabric may occur that is worse than the one caused by alcoholism.

The intervention with the elderly alcoholic needs to take into account the individual's age and capacity to understand. Often the alcoholic's senses are clouded, and the intervention process must be adjusted accordingly. If at all possible, the treatment facility chosen for the individual needs to have staff that specialize in the geriatric alcoholic. Treatment is slower and lasts longer, but it can be extremely effective. I have had the opportunity of doing interventions on alcoholics as old as eighty-three.

Senior citizens have tremendous respect for the professions. Therefore, including a physician and/or a pastor in the intervention is a good idea. Grandchildren can also be extremely helpful in intervening on the elderly. I know of no one who doesn't look forward to his or her years as a grandparent, having made a commitment to be a better grandparent than he or she was a parent. As a result, a special bond between grandparent and grandchild often exists, and the power of that bond expressed in love can help begin the recovery process.

These are the key components of an intervention with the elderly:

1. Gentleness
2. Respect
3. Enough information to get past denial, but not enough to destroy

One also needs to allow the elderly time for recovery. Because of their advanced age, the physical, emotional, and spiritual recovery occur at a much slower pace. If that time is available, they can live out their remaining years with dignity and respect.

Often the intervention with the alcoholic is initiated by those of the adult children who have begun to see the childhood patterns they remember repeated with their children. Frequently the spouses of elderly alcoholics are so enmeshed in the disease and so codependent that it is extremely difficult for them to give themselves permission to take positive action. As a result, we often end up doing two interventions: one with the codependent spouse, followed by one with the alcoholic. A trained interventionist can help the spouse become willing to acknowledge the seriousness of the problem, to stop the cover-up, and to give permission to help resolve a problem that he or she has been living with for years.

The Polyaddicted

One of the sad realities of the these times is that anyone under the age of thirty-five entering treatment today for alcohol or drug addiction is probably dual-dependent. Pure alcoholism is rapidly giving way to polydrug abuse and polydrug addiction. Often we are dealing with chemicals that have contrary effects on the human organism. Within a short period of time the individual can go from depression or lethargy to energy, or from a euphoric giddiness to a deep depression.

The polarizing and imbalancing effects of different chemicals and combinations of chemicals make intervention more difficult and require greater planning and skill from the interventionist. Often it is quite difficult to find a time when the individual is really drug-free. The more complex the disease and the symptomatology, the better planned the intervention must be.

With cocaine use, one often sees great paranoia that gets in the way of the intervention process and causes the addict to perceive love as a threat. Frequently, families and loved ones become frightened by the paranoia, and this fear traps them in the disease and its web of silence instead of motivating them to seek help.

It is not uncommon for those who live with the polyaddicted to feel like prisoners or hostages, constantly fearing for their own safety. As a defense mechanism, many cocaine addicts threaten any family member who tries to stop them. Sometimes the addict may even threaten the lives of others.

Because the cost of the street drugs can be substantial, the family must come to grips with some of the side effects of involvement with such drugs. Secondary aspects of this disease, such as drug dealing, may pose additional dangers for addicts. Also, it is quite common for cocaine addicts to be forced into prostituting themselves in exchange for drugs. This happens not only to female addicts but also to male addicts.

Affected families must view these conditions as symptoms of the disease and not get caught up in emotional responses. Because the combination of mood-altering chemicals presents so many risks, one cannot intervene too soon. The addict's behavior can be complex and confusing. However, this only means that the interventionist must have greater skill and the family must prepare more thoroughly. Quite frequently, there may be drug debts to pay off in order to pave the way for treatment.

Dual Diagnosis

Alcohol and drug dependency continue to affect an ever-larger segment of our population. However, addicts are no more likely to have simultaneous psychiatric disorders than any other segment of the population. The difficulty lies in being able to differentiate between true psychiatric disease and the side effects of polydrug use. A skilled interventionist and clinician will be helpful here. Sometimes, of course, the addict may also suffer from psychiatric disease. This, however, shouldn't stop intervention. Instead, the intervention must be handled with more skill and coupled with a more sophisticated treatment plan. Numerous metropolitan areas around the country have residential treatment facilities that specialize in dual-diagnosis patients.

There are individuals who suffer from psychiatric disease before they develop a chemical dependency. These individuals may have gotten involved with alcohol and drugs to try to relieve the psychiatric disorder. Although that self-medication may have been somewhat successful initially, the psychiatric symptoms quickly are exacerbated. The following major differences exist in interventions for dual-diagnosis patients:

1. A more skilled interventionist is required.
2. Longer and more detailed preparation is required.
3. Intervention takes longer.
4. Intervention is often conducted at a dual-diagnosis hospital facility.

Do not defer intervention because the individual you are concerned about may be suffering from two diseases simultaneously. In fact, because addiction can propel the psychiatric disease to far deeper levels, steps toward intervention ought to proceed as rapidly as possible.

Intervention with Friends

Approximately 7 percent of the interventions I have done did not include family at all. Frequently these interventions occur on the Lost Child of the dysfunctional family, a child who has put a great deal of emotional and geographic distance between himself or herself and his or her family. As a result, the primary family has no knowledge of the alcohol and drug abuse problems. The intervention that occurs with only the friends of the individual can be equally powerful and successful.

Since we are also dealing with a family disease, it is not uncommon that the significant people in the individual's family may also have a problem. At some point, they may need to be eliminated from the intervention because of their own disease. Typically, individuals with such families are young professionals, unmarried or divorced. Coworkers and close personal friends are able to see the effects that the addict's self-destructive course has on the development of his or her career. These friends seek out an interventionist for the same reason that a family does: Somebody they care about deeply is gradually destroying himself or herself.

It is important to emphasize that we are dealing with intervention, not confrontation. With confrontation the power comes from information coupled with ultimatums. In intervention, the power comes from care, concern, and love. When friends care enough to risk a friendship to reach somebody and to help them to help themselves, it communicates a powerful message.

Family is important but certainly not necessary to intervene successfully. If we are dealing with a Lost Child and/or a Scapegoat of a dysfunctional family, often the intervention will be more successful without family. Forcing a reconnection with a distant family may make it more difficult to accept help. Most of all, it is difficult to avoid getting involved in the family dysfunction and to prevent the Scapegoat from focusing on it. The purpose of having family involved in the intervention process is to help bathe the individual in love. If the involvement of the family does not help the individual to feel cared for, we do better to leave family out of the process and use only friends in the intervention.

The Single Parent

Because more than 50 percent of marriages end in divorce, many interventions are done on single parents. As a result of an addiction and a painful divorce, the single parent is often too frightened to seek help, lest the issue of alcoholism or drug addiction be used against them in a custody battle. Although the disease and preparation for intervention may be the same, frequently the single parent must face a difficult issue: "What will happen to my children while I am in treatment?"

These individuals are usually relatively young, so the risks of dual addiction are quite high. Especially when coupled with cocaine, the addiction frequently causes great paranoia. The dual-addicted, paranoid single parent may regard the request to accept treatment as a ploy to take the children away.

Such parents also may be very afraid that the noncustodial parent will try to use the addiction to gain custody.

These individuals are truly in a double bind. If they do nothing to take care of their disease, they may eventually find themselves in trouble with the law. If they do nothing the disease will provide sufficient ammunition for custody fights. But if they do enter treatment, an angry former spouse may attempt to turn this positive step against them in a custody battle.

Carefully structured and planned interventions can, for the most part, lessen these risks. By working closely with the treatment facility, the single parent often can be allowed to have additional contact with his or her children. This helps allay the fear that somehow the extended family is trying to take the children away.

If it appears likely that custody may become an issue it may be advisable to have legal counsel involved in the intervention process. For example, the attorney who handled the divorce and custody agreement can help advise the prospective patient of the risks and how to minimize them. Counsel also can help advise the prospective patient of the risks of doing nothing.

Do not allow potential difficulties, even major ones, to prevent you from consulting an interventionist. A skilled interventionist can help deal with the obstacles and difficulties presented by the particular circumstances of the case. Doing nothing or denying the addiction is far riskier.

A basic rule of intervention is that the more difficult it may be to get an individual to accept help, the more planning must be done prior to the intervention. But if the structure of the intervention has been planned, the intervention can be just as successful as any other.

Interventions in Families
with More Than One Chemically
Dependent Person

Having more than one chemically dependent person in a family is not at all uncommon because we are dealing with a disease with a pronounced genetic component. Those sharing the disease may be siblings, spouses, or others. This circumstance should not stop you from proceeding with the intervention.

The skilled interventionist can help you assess where to start. Frequently I prefer to start with the individual who is most likely to succeed. In doing that first intervention, we eliminate from the process other persons who are chemically dependent in order to minimize the risk of sabotage. This is especially true if we are dealing with siblings, or a child and a parent.

After you have succeeded in getting the first individual to accept treatment, your interventionist can help determine a course of action for dealing with other addicted members of the family.

Two principal courses of action are frequently followed. If possible, the second intervention may be done immediately after the first. This is almost always a good idea in the case of spouses. We will intervene first with the spouse who is going to be the easiest and most straightforward, and then immediately after intervene with the other. If possible, we may ask the subject of the first intervention to participate in the second one. This must be done in a way that is positive and nonenabling. Frequently, participation will consist of simply saying, "This group has talked to me.

I've decided that I do have a problem and I have made a decision to enter treatment. Would you please enter a companion program so that we can deal with this thing together?" If properly structured and planned by your interventionist, this strategy is almost sure to be successful.

Most treatment facilities do not allow people from the same family, whether siblings or spouses, to be in the same program at the same time. The only exception might be in a facility so large that people can be well separated during treatment. The reason for this is that family members tend to focus on the relationship and family difficulties rather than on their own recovery. However, a companion program may be found that can complement the other treatment program so that there is some joint recovery. Joint post-treatment planning is also important.

When it is not possible or advisable to do the second intervention immediately, often that intervention can occur as a part of the treatment of the primary patient. Most good treatment facilities today incorporate intensive family involvement. As a result, a second or third patient in the same family can often be very successfully intervened on as a part of the family program. Sometimes the new patient can simply take the bed of the patient when he or she has completed treatment.

Multiple alcoholics and addicts in the same family simply require multiple interventions. With one particular family we did six interventions—four on adult children, one on a parent, and one on a stepparent.

Intervention on
Other Compulsive Disorders:
Sexual Addiction

This book is primarily about intervention on alcoholism and drug addiction. We have, however, touched upon other compulsive disorders as well. If you have read this book up to this point you have discovered that each and every addiction has its victims. There is no such thing as a victimless addiction. The addictive disease does not exist in a vacuum. It leaves in its wake broken hearts and fractured spirits and causes the development of a host of unhealthy coping skills. No addictive disorder does that more profoundly and completely than sexual addiction. Sexual addiction not only creates victims but a sense of shame. Just as a sense of shame develops within alcoholics or addicts and their families, so it is prevalent—but even more so—among sexual addicts and their families.

Viewing compulsive sexual acting out as an addictive disorder is relatively new. The first major work published in this area was *Out of the Shadows* by Patrick Carnes, Ph.D., in 1983. His second book, *Contrary to Love*, published in 1989, is an even more complete description of the concept of sexual addiction. Where the alcoholic uses alcohol to help him or her cope with life, to avoid feelings, and to deal with stress, the sex addict oftentimes begins using sex in the same way. What was once a natural expression of love within a committed relationship now becomes clouded and the partner begins to feel confused, torn, and used.

As with all addictions there is a progression from the use of another person or oneself to medicate feelings and avoid problems. It may well progress to a pattern of chronic masturbation in which the individual addict will masturbate at least daily and frequently multiple times daily.

One of the unique components of sexual addiction that separates it from all others is that sexual addicts have within them a driving force to continually increase the risks that they will take. The risk-taking behavior tends to cause as great a rush for them as does a needle in the arm for a drug addict. It is when that risk-taking behavior begins to occur that tremendous difficulties can result, whether that behavior takes the form of open involvement with prostitutes, public exhibitionism or voyeurism, or pedophilia.

Within the home itself the disease of sexual addiction causes deep hurt and profound confusion for everyone who is near it. The absence of overt sexual abuse does not mean that sexual abuse is not occurring. Often there will be excess nudity in the home, which the addict will rationalize by proclaiming the healthiness of an "open family." The addict's behavior frequently will take the form of violation of boundaries for all members of the family by not allowing privacy in the bathroom or in the shower. Children are just as traumatized by inappropriate sexual talk, verbal references to genitalia, and inappropriate sexual jokes as they are by having been fondled or penetrated.

As with the alcoholic and drug addict, the defense mechanisms of rationalization and justification are present. If the sex addict is confronted about: inappropriate sexual talk; sexual jokes; excessive nudity; boundary violations; use of pornography materials such as books and videos; the addict will have a rationalization and a justification for each. When those defense mechanisms fail, like the alcoholic's, the addict will become defensive and begin to blame and attack the confronter for being a prude, old-fashioned, or religious.

Addictive disease of any kind does tremendous damage to those who live with it. Everyone in the family system feels a sense of shame. In our culture we remain rather closed about our sexuality and our sexual self. It is not a subject that we are able to talk about openly. Add to our cultural shame the shame that comes from sexual addiction and we have a web of secrecy that is woven so tightly that almost no one can break out of it. Thus the disease becomes multigenerational before someone breaks the silence.

The shame felt by alcoholics and their families or by drug addicts and their families is a thimbleful as compared to the cargo of a super tanker when we look at sexual addiction and its effect upon the family system. A child who grows up with untreated sexual addiction will need years of therapy to be able to develop a healthy self-esteem and have a healthy relationship.

Intervention on Sex Addicts

Unless intervention occurs early on in the progression of the sexual addiction it is rare that the family or the spouse will initiate the intervention process. As sexual addiction progresses the family's own disease of codependency or coaddiction progresses to the point where they are so caught up in the web of secrecy and shame that they are unable to initiate the intervention process.

Since the concept of sexual addiction itself is rather new we do not have a large body of data on interventions on sex addicts to call upon, and as far as I know there are few if any besides myself doing interventions on sexual addiction. Based on interventions that have been done on sexual addiction, some common denominators with other interventions do exist, as well as some differences.

Intervention is usually initiated by someone outside the family system because sex addicts have drawn attention to their behavior through the legal system, their employers, leaders in their church, or leaders in their profession. Interventions initiated by a family member have been a result of someone in that family system seeking professional help for himself or herself. Adult children in therapy who recognize that part of the baggage they carry is some form of sexual abuse by a parent often feel a therapeutic need to confront the perpetrator. If handled properly, this can be a catalyst to intervention. Spouses who have initiated intervention have done so as a result of receiving therapy and being involved in S-Anon, the family support group for spouses and family members of sex addicts.

If there are family members involved in the intervention process for the sex addicts, the preparation time is considerably longer to allow time to process the personal pain involved. Because the pain and wounding are so deep, one must carefully evaluate the efficacy of having victims of the sex addict involved in the intervention process. If sex addicts are in therapy the therapists need to be duly advised so they have the opportunity to consult with their patient and help determine the appropriateness of their involvement.

With other interventions, we have spoken of how important the expression of love and genuine care about the individual is. With sexual addiction often there are too many wounds for individual family members to be able to state their love in any kind of honest way. Rather than beginning the presentation of their data with, "Dad, I am here today because I love you," they begin by saying, "I am here today to tell you about a problem that you have and its effects upon me." Whether or not the ability to express the feelings of care will return largely depends upon the response of the sex addict and how beneficial treatment is. Not only is the wounding of the family system so deep that family members frequently are unable to express care or love, but their response to the pain can be most severe. As I stated earlier, the data base is not large at this point, but it is not uncommon for the loved ones of the sex addict to feel the pain so deeply that they have significant physiological responses. They may feel faint, they may need to leave the room, or they may need to vomit.

Interventions that have been done on sex addicts have been extremely successful. It may be that the reason for this success is different than for the alcoholic or drug addict. Much of the success of intervention on the alcoholic or addict hinges upon the love that is expressed as well as the individuals who are participating in the intervention. If the alcoholic or addict truly respects and cares for the individuals involved, the chances for success are immense. With sexual addiction, however, it appears that the largest contributing factor to success is getting rid of the secret. The sex addicts themselves are overwhelmed with shame and guilt. Simply letting them know that you know what is going on with them and that their secret behavior is no longer a secret may well be the largest contributing factor to successful intervention and the onset of treatment.

There are now several residential treatment centers for sexual addiction around the country. Excellent help is available both for the addict and for the family itself.

Current estimates by Dr. Carnes and other leaders in the field of sexual addiction indicate that 6 to 8 percent of our population suffer from sexual addiction. Though that is small in comparison to the percentage of alcoholics and drug addicts in our country, I feel it is far too significant a population to ignore, both for treatment as well as for the intervention process, which is critical for all addictive diseases. Sexual addicts and their families need help. Intervention works but it is only the first step in the long course of treatment, both for the addict as well as for the family members.

Failed Interventions

No matter the degree of expertise of your interventionist there will be those interventions, though small in number, that fail completely! The alcoholic or addict in no uncertain terms will not allow himself or herself to receive any kind of help. However, all is not lost.

Even when the addicted person has refused help in the interventions I have been involved with over the past years, almost without exception much has been gained. Many treatment centers around the country will allow the family of the alcoholic who refuses help through intervention to participate in the family program as though the patient were there. As a result of their participation in the family program, the participants have begun to get help for themselves. Irrespective of what the alcoholic or addict does, you as a spouse or as a child can live a far healthier life as a result of having broken the secret and sought help.

The adult children in the family system often will enter therapy for their own issues and for the healing of their own pain as a result of the intervention process, even though the intervention itself may have failed. Frequently spouses of alcoholics who refused treatment will enter therapy for themselves so that they can cope with life in a healthier way.

So even in failure there can be tremendous success. The worst possible outcome is that your conscience will be clear because you will know you have tried and you as an individual can begin your own recovery. That is a lot of success out of failure, and that in and of itself ought to be reason enough to try.

Intervention
Following Failed Intervention

It is not uncommon for family and friends to try to intervene without the help of a trained interventionist and fail. Because of this, these families are often reluctant to intervene again. However, professionally guided and structured intervention can be successful in spite of a previous failure.

Although second interventions are difficult, I am frequently faced with them, and I often succeed. The failure of a previous intervention, with or without the help of a professional, is no reason to give up. We wouldn't give up with any other disease, and I don't believe we ought to give up with the disease of addiction, either.

7

Ending the Cycle of Codependency

Codependents are spouses and significant others involved in a relationship with the chemically dependent. The subject of codependency is a broad one. At its root is how we as a society have developed and how we as an extended family reinforce unhealthy caretaking behavior.

Because this book is primarily about intervention, it is not intended to be all-encompassing in its look at codependency. For those who wish to pursue a more exhaustive study of codependency, some excellent material has been written in the last few years. Anne Wilson Schaef's works, *When Society Becomes an Addict* and *Co-Dependence: Misunderstood, Mistreated* are as solid as they come, and Melody Beattie's *Codependent No More* provides a thorough understanding of the codependent disorder.

I call it a disorder because like the disease of addiction it has identifiable symptomatology coupled with a progressive course that ultimately renders the codependent as helpless as the alcoholic. If you are in a primary relationship with someone affected with the disease of chemical dependency, then you are codependent and at risk for developing as many difficulties and health problems as the chemically dependent person. Each day that your codependency goes unchecked and untreated, you lose some of your ability to relate in an emotionally healthy way and to be emotionally present in the here and now.

Codependents are not bad people doing bad things. Rather, they are unhealthy people caring for others in unhealthy ways. They are the loved ones of alcoholics and addicts and other dysfunctional individuals caring and caretaking for them in a way that does not work. They are often beautiful people with beautiful motives whose methods do not get the job done. They are individuals with their own faulty belief systems, individuals whose own defense mechanisms get in the way of proper care and support, individuals whose own sense of self-worth and self-esteem are lacking.

Until now this book has spoken primarily of alcoholics and addicts and their disease and dysfunction. One of the key points made earlier in this work was that because of this disease and dysfunction, the individual lacks objectivity adequately to assess and treat the disorder. This chapter is about you, the loved one of the alcoholic and addict, and because it is about you, you will naturally have difficulty being objective. Do not expect yourself to be totally objective, and give yourself permission to receive input and guidance in understanding this important aspect of yourself.

The disorder of codependency is not unlike that of addiction. The codependent develops his or her own belief system similar to that of the chemically dependent person. Let us review the belief system of the alcoholic:

1. I know there is a problem but . . .
2. Nobody would understand.
3. No one could possibly accept me or the changes I need to make.
4. But I am different.
5. I'm stuck—what's the use.

The spouse or significant other of the alcoholic or addict gets caught up in that belief and denial system and begins to use the defense mechanisms of excusing, rationalizing, and justifying the disorder. Compounding this belief system is the codependent's lack of a feeling of self-worth, which causes him or her to add supporting data to the belief system. The codependent begins to think perhaps he or she is at least partially responsible for the problem. The thinking goes like this:

Maybe if I'd . . .
    tried harder
    cared more
    not gotten angry
    spent money
    not spent money
    had sex
    not had sex
    been home
    not been home
    kept the kids quiet
    let the kids play
    prayed
    gone to church
    invited family
    not invited family
    been stronger
    etc., etc., etc.

Yes, there is a problem. But I should have been . . .

slicker
quicker
smarter
brighter

And if I had been, it wouldn't be that bad and probably would have gone away. If I had been . . .
a better parent
a better child
a better lover
it probably would not have gotten out of hand.

The belief that another's chemical dependency is, at least in part, your own fault is really a false omnipotence. You do not have the power to force someone to make unhealthy choices on a daily basis. You do not and did not have the power to cause disease.

The belief that no one could possibly understand the problem and that if they did understand they would not accept it is equally powerful. This aspect of the belief system, like the first, combines the feelings and the beliefs of the alcoholic or the addict with your own erosion of self-esteem and self-worth. That combination places you in a double-bind position. First, you believe that others could not understand or accept that the one you love has a problem. Second, you believe that if others could understand or accept that there is a problem, they would be inclined to blame you for not having done more to prevent it and more to protect your loved one.

Once we understand that all the things we as codependents did to try to protect and take care of the alcoholic or addict were in essence enabling behaviors, we put ourselves in a double bind by saying that no one could understand or accept how much we have enabled, no one could possibly accept or understand how codependent we have become.

The result is that we are stuck, slowly but steadily progressing to a life of more and more secrecy, more and more cover-up, more and more shame. Our denial becomes as strong as the denial of the alcoholic or addict. Our minimizing is strong, and our inability to see the elephant grows. Our sense of hopelessness and our sense of denial grow in equal proportion, and so the diseases of addiction and codependency grow. As the diseases grow, we isolate more, and as we isolate we feel more lost, lonely, frustrated, angry, and helpless. As we feel more lost we keep more and more inside, and so our senses of self-worth and self-esteem erode. And as our self-esteem diminishes, we lose the ability to be spontaneous and emotionally present in the here and now.

We begin to live life like a rehearsal. We continually rehearse in our minds upcoming events: "If he or she does this I will respond like this." "If he or she does that I will respond like that." We rehearse daily the next potential problem, the next potential crisis, the next situation, rehearsing not one option but two or three or four to prepare for various behaviors and actions of the other person:

Carefully calculating
Carefully strategizing to try to control the uncontrollable
Managing the unmanageable and reasoning with the irrational

To begin to end the cycle of codependency, you must ask yourself questions that go to the roots of self-worth:

1. Am I worth a relationship with someone whose primary relationship is with me, not with alcohol or drugs (or work, gambling, food, sex)?
2. Am I worth a relationship with someone who is capable of being emotionally present on a consistent basis?
3. Am I worth a relationship in which I do not have to excuse, rationalize, justify, cover up, or keep secret someone's behavior?
4. Am I worth a relationship in which I do not have to expend my emotional energy in rehearsing?
5. Am I worth a relationship that promises more than another crisis?
6. Am I worth a relationship that is void of blame?
7. Am I worth a relationship in which I am able to care for and about rather than having to take care of?
8. Am I worth a relationship in which I do not need to walk on eggshells?
9. Am I worth a relationship in which I do not need to feel guilty?
10. Am I worth a relationship void of fear?

Ending the cycle of codependency does not have to do with the alcoholic or addict and his or her problem, disease, and behavior. Rather, it has to do with you and your self-worth. I hope that you can discover that you are worth all of the above and much, much more. If you can, then it becomes possible for you to be a powerful force in the intervention process. If you doubt that you have a right to the things on the self-worth list, then your participation in intervention will be prone to enabling. Your interventionist can guide you over this hurdle, so don't let your doubt stop you from getting started.

Earlier in this book we discussed the belief system that evolves in the chemically dependent person as well as in the codependent. We also spoke of the dual personality system, or the A and B sides, of the chemically dependent person. A similar tool exists with the codependent.

The A Side (The Codependent Side)

Lets others' wants, desires, and values override one's own

Rationalizes and justifies each override as a special circumstance

Internally promises that next time will be different, but is unable to stick to it or can be talked out of it

Lets others' opinions override and become more important than one's opinion of oneself

Secretly blames oneself or others for the difficulties occurring as a result of alcoholism or drug addiction

The B Side (The Core Side)

Has a strong set of goals, values, and beliefs for marriage, children, etc.

When I get married I will not tolerate . . .
When I have children I will not tolerate . . .
Holidays are going to be . . .
I will not allow my children to be exposed to . . .
I will not allow myself to be treated . . .

Codependents or chief enabling persons generally grew up in dysfunctional families. As a result of that experience they made strong commitments to creating lives for themselves and their families different from those they experienced. Living with addiction, however, causes a gradual but steady erosion of those commitments and beliefs.

To begin breaking the cycle of addiction and codependency, it is important for you to have a basic awareness of how enmeshed in the disorder you have become. As a result of that enmeshment you have moved further and further away from your true self and have become more and more codependent.

In the codependent pattern of living people develop behaviors—conscious and unconscious—that enable the alcoholic and addict to maintain a destructive pattern. Although their motives may be noble, enabling behavior helps to foster and nurture the disease. The motives may be those of attempting to keep the peace and trying to prevent the problem from getting worse, but in the end the opposite occurs.

The following partial list of codependent and enabling behaviors will help you to get in touch with how the disease of addiction has affected you and how you have silently enabled it to continue. I have left room for you to make notes about each of your enabling behaviors.

In what ways have I protected and covered up for the chemically dependent person?

From family _____

_____

_____

_____

_____

From friends _____

_____

_____

_____

_____

From the children _____

_____

_____

_____

_____

From the employer _____

_____

_____

_____

As the chief enabler of the chemically dependent person you cover up by cancelling events, apologizing for not showing up, and coming up with excuses for not being present at family functions or social engagements. When going to social engagements where there is a risk that the one you are concerned about may let his or her drinking get out of control, you work hard before you leave at trying to elicit promises in an effort to control the amount of drinking so that others will not see the difficulties. You apologize to the children and make excuses to them for the other parent's behavior, but never quite tell them the truth. You may call the employer to say that your spouse is sick.

What secrets have I promised to keep? Part of our codependent and enabling behavior is the keeping of secrets.

From extended family _____

_____

_____

_____

_____

From church groups _____

_____

_____

_____

_____

_____

From neighbors_____

_____

_____

_____

_____

_____

From friends_____

_____

_____

_____

_____

_____

From the children_____

_____

_____

_____

_____

_____

What excuses have I used to cover up?

Addiction causes both the individual and the family affected
with the disease to feel a great deal of shame. Frequently
it is those embarrassing and shame-filled actions that cause
us to keep secrets. Think of times when you or the chemically dependent person felt especially embarrassed or
ashamed. Think of the secrets that you have been keeping.
Write them down either in the space provided or in a separate notebook.

_____

_____

_____

_____

_____

_____

_____

_____

_____

_____

What beliefs and values have I slowly compromised as a result of my relationship with the alcoholic or addict? By being codependent slowly but steadily my own values and belief systems erode.

_____

_____

_____

_____

_____

_____

_____

_____

_____

_____

Historically what were my attitudes toward drunk driving, use of cocaine and marijuana, dealing of drugs? What were my attitudes toward emotional abuse of children? How have I compromised those values?

_____

_____

_____

_____

_____

_____

_____

_____

_____

How have I compromised my religious values and my religious activities?
Frequently because of embarrassment and shame about chemical dependency, codependents move away from their church support groups.

_____

_____

_____

_____

_____

_____

_____

_____

_____

How have I compromised my sexual values?

Spouses of alcoholic or chemically dependent persons consistently report that it is painful to attempt to make love with someone who is intoxicated. They feel used and frequently feel that they are dirty. The result is not a love relationship and shared intimacy but uncomfortable and often emotionally painful sex.

_____

_____

_____

_____

_____

_____

_____

_____

_____

_____

What boundaries have I set and then later backed away from?

One of the things that family members of alcoholics and addicts frequently do is to set up boundaries on behavior that results from addiction. They tell the chemically dependent person that certain things should not occur again and that if they do, they promise that they will take some specific action.

If he or she drinks and drives again, I'll_____

_____

_____

_____

_____

_____

If he or she gets drunk again, I'll_____

_____

_____

_____

_____

_____

If he or she gets stoned again, I'll_____

_____

_____

_____

_____

If he or she breaks things again, I'll_____

_____

_____

_____

_____

If the children get hurt again, I'll_____

_____

_____

_____

_____

_____

If the children get scared again, I'll_____

_____

_____

_____

_____

If this happens on the holidays again, I'll_____

_____

_____

_____

_____

What commitments have I made to myself and/or to others that things were going to change, that the pattern of problems was going to be broken, and that I would not tolerate it any longer?

It doesn't matter whether these boundaries were shared with the other person or were simply part of your dialogue with yourself.

It is very important for you to understand that in doing this brief inventory of your codependent and enabling behaviors you are not dealing with patterns that are right or wrong, good or bad. Enabling and codependent behaviors are symptoms of the disease. The purpose of this evaluation is simply to help you to become aware of how enmeshed and pervasive the disease has become and to develop an understanding of its effects on you and the entire family system. What have occurred are not mistakes but symptoms, not screw-ups but the pervasiveness of the disease.

Now that you have an understanding of addiction and alcoholism and how they progress, of codependency and how it progresses, and of loving intervention, you are ready to proceed with specific preparation for the process of intervention.

8

Choosing an
Interventionist

Unfortunately there is no professional organization of interventionists and there are no established criteria for assessing their training. As a result, many people who do interventions have had little or no training at all, and so the quality of their services varies considerably. I hope that this work will encourage the establishment of a national association of interventionists which can begin setting some standards for education and ongoing training. These standards will determine criteria that professional interventionists will have to meet to become certified.

However, until such standards are set we must deal with the current situation. Do not be afraid to ask your interventionist some very pointed questions about how many interventions he or she has done. What was the success rate? What training has he or she received in interventions? In the fields of chemical dependency and psychology?

Not only must interventionists have a solid academic background in the area of addictions, but they ought also to have some very specific psychotherapy training. The psychotherapy training will help them to have the appropriate attitude towards defense mechanisms. Defense mechanisms need to be respected and worked with rather than confronted judgmentally. Without such training, interventionists may want to rely on confrontation, and though they may be successful in getting your loved one to enter treatment, they may create as many problems as they solve.

Training in the fields of addictions and psychotherapy is only part of what is required. Interventionists must also have excellent assessment skills, since part of the task of the interventionist is to do a comprehensive assessment of the chemically dependent person and his or her related psychological problems without ever having seen him or her. This is very difficult and requires well-developed assessment skills for alcohol and drug addiction as well as for other psychological conditions.

These may seem like very high standards. I believe, however, that they ought to be minimum ones. Unfortunately, many people doing interventions today do not have this kind of training and would be unable to meet the standards that I have outlined. As a result you may have to settle for less than ideal treatment.

Here are some key questions for you to consider when selecting the interventionist who will work best for you:

1. What primary training in addictions have they received?
2. What primary training in psychotherapy have they received?

3. What primary training in intervention have they received?
4. How many interventions have they done?
5. What is their success rate?
6. What types of interventions have they done? Here are some specific categories:
   Alcohol
   Drugs
   A combination of alcohol and drugs
   Dual diagnosis
   Food addiction and other eating disorders
   Workaholism
   Codependency
   Gambling

7. Do they recommend that families do the intervention on their own after preparation? If they do, look elsewhere.
8. Do they rely on ultimatums? If they do, they are still caught up in the confrontation style of intervention, and this indicates a lack of broad-based training.
9. Are they familiar with this book? If they have not read it, I would encourage you to insist that they do. Afterwards, sit down with them to see whether or not they will immediately adjust their style of intervention.
10. Do they receive compensation from the treatment facilities they refer to?

Asking these kinds of questions can only increase your comfort with and confidence in your interventionist. The majority of these questions do not require elaboration here because they have been addressed in some form in other parts of this book. Be sure that your interventionist does have some specific experience that matches your particular situation.

I do wish to elaborate, however, on the last two questions. Because the style of intervention I propose, which basically avoids confrontation and ultimatums, is new, the interventionist you choose may not be familiar with it. If he or she has broad-based training and has read this book, the results will be most favorable. If after reading this book he or she still seems to want to use confrontation or sees no reason why the family cannot do this on their own I encourage you to find another interventionist. However, the mere fact that he or she has not had an opportunity to read this book ought not to disqualify him or her.

Whether or not the interventionist you are working with receives compensation from treatment facilities is also quite important. Many treatment centers around the country provide free interventions. Often the interventionist's primary responsibility is to market the treatment center, and he or she is one of the key individuals primarily responsible for filling the treatment facility's beds. If that is the interventionist's primary responsibility, then I believe he or she will find it difficult to be totally objective about your situation and your loved one's therapeutic needs. You need not disqualify someone merely because he or she is part of a treatment facility. But the interventionist should be candid about his or her role and flexible about which treatment facility you choose. If you are not sure, get a second opinion.

No single treatment center is ideal for every situation. Every facility has its strengths and weaknesses. How well it works depends upon the specific situation. It is very important that an interventionist who works as part of a staff and receives his or her compensation from a treatment facility be free to allow your loved one to enter another facility when that seems best.

There are also interventionists who may not appear to have a direct connection with a treatment facility, but who nevertheless receive compensation from a treatment facility for having referred patients. Again, this sets up a potential conflict of interest. The more removed your interventionist is from specific treatment facilities, and the more he or she bases referrals on patients' needs, the more objective he or she is likely to be.

It is my fondest hope that soon we will develop training and experience criteria that can provide the basis for a certification process for interventionists. Ethical standards must also be set to ensure the interventionist's objectivity. Until these standards are enforced, however, you must be a smart consumer.

Most regions of the country have alcohol and drug resource information centers. Treatment centers in your region also can make specific referrals based upon their experience with trained interventionists. There are also interventionists like myself who will travel far and wide to do interventions that require special expertise.

Though there is no official national organization of interventionists, I maintain a sizable file of names of interventionists in different regions of the country. The treatment facilities or employee-assistance program personnel in your area should have access to such a list as well.

9

Choosing a
Treatment Facility

It would be most unfortunate indeed to have spent much time and money on a successful intervention only to have your loved one treated in an inappropriate or substandard facility.

Unless one has had some firsthand experience with specialized treatment for addictions, the mere mention of treatment conjures up many negative images. It is amazing to me that people still view treatment facilities as institutions that have padded rooms, restraints, and locked doors. Many also view treatment facilities as places that force the patients to drink alcohol and then force them to vomit. This so-called aversion therapy, popular in the 1950s and 1960s, has been eliminated from the treatment field.

As part of the intervention process it is important that you develop confidence in the treatment facility your loved one will enter. Your interventionist often will make some very specific recommendations based on the treatment needs that he or she sees. However, you ought to visit the facility yourself so that you can overcome your fears about residential treatment.

It is also important to believe that this is the best treatment center for your situation. To help you be an informed consumer, here are some specific points to consider and questions to ask the treatment center:

1. **What is the program's philosophy? Are alcoholism and drug addiction considered to be physical diseases?**

   In spite of all that has been written to date about the diseases of alcoholism and drug addiction, some facilities still view addiction as a symptom of an underlying psychological or psychiatric problem. This is true only in some cases of dual diagnoses. Even in such cases, however, the addiction needs to be treated as primary. Since this matter is a philosophical one, I encourage you to ask whatever questions you need to ask to be satisfied that the program considers addiction to be a physical disease. For example, do the medical director or other staff members give lectures to their patients about the medical aspects of this disease? Does the treatment facility focus more on medical aspects of recovery or on detox? For example, do they educate patients and encourage them to change their diets and levels of physical activity?

2. **How is detoxification managed?**

   Contrary to popular belief only a small percentage of individuals admitted to residential treatment facilities for alcohol- or drug-related problems are going to have medically serious detoxification difficulties. Since, however, the possibility of severe life-threatening withdrawal does always exist when we are dealing with alcohol and other addictions, it is most important that the detoxification staff be specially trained in the management of withdrawal and that they be under the close supervision of the medical director.

Visit the detoxification section of the treatment facility and develop comfort with and confidence in the staff.

3. **Who is the medical director and what specialized training in addictions does that individual have?** A medical specialty has developed in recent years called addictionology. Many medical directors have studied this specialty. If the medical director of the treatment facility you have selected is an addictionologist, you can rest assured that his or her training in the management of addictions is first-rate. However, because it is a relatively new specialty the medical director of the treatment facility that you choose may not yet have mastered this field. That does not mean that he or she is not qualified or specially trained. Nevertheless, be a smart consumer, particularly if your interventionist feels that the patient may have a difficult detox. Ask whatever questions you need to ask in order to feel comfortable. As a result, you will often discover medical directors who have been treated for this disease and therefore have a wealth of personal experience as well as considerable professional expertise.

4. **What ancillary medical care is available if your loved one develops complications?**
Many quality treatment facilities available today are freestanding facilities; that is, they are physically separate from hospitals. In itself, this poses no problem. They should, however, have an arrangement with a nearby hospital for emergency medical care should it be needed. Asking questions about emergency medical care can help to reassure you.

5. **Are the Twelve Step Programs of Alcoholics Anonymous, Cocaine Anonymous, and Al-Anon an integral and mandatory part of the treatment process?**
Community-based support groups such as Alcoholics Anonymous, Cocaine Anonymous, and Al-Anon may evoke stereotypical images just as treatment does. You may not understand how critical it is that your loved one be involved in the Twelve Step Programs. Rest assured, though, that such involvement is totally essential to long-term recovery.

The treatment facility ought to be doing a great deal more than paying lip service to these programs. When you look at the treatment facility's daily and weekly schedule, you ought to see a number of A.A. meetings held either at the facility or in the community. Transportation should be provided if the meetings are not held at the facility.

The daily schedule should also indicate patients' schedules for working through various aspects of the Twelve Step Programs. Many top-quality treatment centers will try to move patients through the first five steps. At the very least, the patient, before leaving treatment, ought thoroughly to understand at least the first three steps. Those who do not become involved in the Twelve Step Programs during treatment probably will not make them a part of their life after treatment. And those who fail to do so tend quickly to relapse.

6. **Is there a clergy staff that is an integral part of the treatment team?**
   Earlier we spoke about the need for the treatment facilities to view alcoholism and drug addiction as physical diseases. Equally important, something must be done to remedy the spiritual depletion that occurs with addiction. Specially trained clergy can help patients to reconnect with a power greater than themselves. If specially trained clergy are not an integral part of the team, then there is a good chance the treatment philosophy is not at all compatible with the Twelve Step Programs.

7. **What are the training and qualifications of the counseling staff?**
   Though this may be difficult to assess, don't be afraid to ask some pointed questions about the qualifications of the on-line counseling staff. These are the staff individuals who will spend by far the greatest amount of time with you and your loved one and so will have the greatest impact upon the addict and subsequently his or her recovery.
       For a long time, the field has relied on putting recovery individuals through a six-month or one-year

training program to teach them beginning counseling skills, and then putting them in charge of groups in a treatment facility. Trying to run a treatment facility staffed only by counselors with such minimal qualifications, however, is like trying to run a medical hospital staffed only by LPNs and nurse's aides.

It is to be hoped that the treatment facility you are visiting will have on-line counseling staff members with more training than the standard one-year program provides. More and more treatment facilities are requiring their counselors to have at least a bachelor's degree, and many have a master's degree in counseling or psychology. It also is important to find out the extent to which those without higher degrees are supervised.

8. Do the staff and the facility meet any sort of certification requirements?

Many states today require alcohol and drug counselors to go through a state certification process. National organizations may also provide certification. Maintaining certification requires continuing education. If you discover that a number of the staff have specialized certification, you can rest assured that they are probably also getting some ongoing training.

There are also accrediting bodies for the treatment facilities themselves. One of the most widely known and accepted is the Joint Commission on the Accreditation of Healthcare Organizations, known as JCAHO. Accreditation by such national organizations indicates that the institution is meeting a national and widely accepted standard of care. I recall most vividly the site visits by the accreditation team during my years as a therapist in a residential treatment facility. Though these accreditation teams may be hard on the treatment staff, I have always found them to be helpful. Following each accreditation visit, I believe the quality of treatment improved. Such accreditation indicates a dedication to high standards and a commitment to quality care.

9. To what extent are psychological evaluation and staff involvement available?

This is not only a physical disease but also a disease with many psychological and emotional side effects. Involving trained psychologists is as important as involving clergy. In many treatment facilities around the country, the psychologist and medical director are people that buzz in and buzz out of the treatment facility and are not involved in the day-to-day care of the patient. This level of involvement is insufficient.

Besides doing a detailed psychological profile and evaluation, the psychologist ought to be involved in the therapeutic planning meetings, which should occur at least once a week. You should be cautious about choosing any facility where psychologists are less involved.

10. What is the ratio of staff to patients?

Since much of the healing that occurs will take place in daily counseling groups, the ratio of staff to patients needs to be sufficiently high. If the on-line counselors conduct groups of more than eight patients, the quality of care will suffer and recovery will be more difficult. Certainly the number of patients may fluctuate, and sometimes the ratio may be exceeded for a short period of time. However, this ought to be the exception rather than the norm.

11. **What is the mix of the patient population? Are different social groups represented or does the patient population tend to be homogeneous?**
Professionals have debated for years the pros and cons of creating programs designed for specific populations. Such programs are highly specialized, dealing only with adolescents, women, professionals, clergy, and so on.

However, adolescents are the only group that seems to have significantly different needs. For the most part, adolescents in treatment have gotten themselves in a great deal of difficulty academically, and part of the treatment involves creating an environment that supports academic activity. Also, because of their different level of emotional maturity, often adolescents have a difficult time blending in with the therapeutic groups that are an essential part of treatment.

Beyond that exception, I much prefer to see a mix of patients: men, women, gays, professionals, factory workers. The beliefs that develop as a part of this disease emphasize uniqueness and difference. "I am unique," the patient says, "I am different." Setting up special programs for particular groups encourages this unhealthy way of thinking.

This is not to say that being a woman or a professional or a gay person does not involve special problems. However, these problems can be addressed by special groups within the structured treatment process and later by post-treatment care. The instances of this disease have more similarities than differences, and I believe we do better not to isolate the patient or to encourage the belief in his or her uniqueness.

12. **Most important, what program does the treatment facility offer for the family?**
If the program for the family is less than a week long, look for another facility. Also, more and more treatment facilities are recognizing that treating the patient alone without addressing the damage caused to the family is a sure way to fail. Some years ago a professional experienced in the field of chemical dependency said that if it were up to him, he would admit the entire family. The only difference in treatment would be that the family members would not need detox. This indicates the amount of recovery required for everyone close to the chemically dependent person.

Quality treatment centers today are offering four and a half- to five-day intensive family treatment as a part of the treatment process for the primary patient. This must include more than education. Part of the process must involve an opportunity to address some of the damage that has occurred and to begin a recovery process for the individual family members and the family unit. It must also involve the development, with the guidance of the family therapist, of a specific treatment plan for family members' own long-term recovery.

13. **After discharge, what ongoing care is provided by the facility for treatment?**
The time that the patient and family spend in the intensive-treatment facility is but phase one of the treatment and recovery process. Continuing care and therapy, either at the facility or with a specially trained private addictions counselor, are immensely important. If treatment stops the day the patient is discharged, the chances of long-term success decrease. This phase of the treatment is as important as the residential phase.

14. **How does the facility deal with ACoA (Adult Children of Alcoholics) and codependency issues?**
We are dealing with a genetic disease, and in many cases with multiple generations of family dysfunction. It is important to address the therapeutic issues that arise from the multigenerational dysfunction. For years, experts in the chemical dependence field have believed that treatment should not deal with the issues of being an adult child of an alcoholic or a codependent until the patient has been in recovery for a year.

I know of no viable research that has been done to support this view. On the contrary, failing to address immediately some of the major issues adult children of alcoholics face can make staying sober next to impossible. I believe that this is especially true when these issues involve physical or sexual abuse. Much good material has been written about this over the last several years. Many victims are filled with shame that results from an abusive upbringing, and so they have been caught in a lifelong cycle of self-sabotage. Unless they can deal with these issues through intensive psychotherapy, they may well sabotage their recovery. Recovery from alcohol and drug addiction and recovery from dysfunctional families need not exclude each other.

15. Why residential treatment only?

This book addresses those situations, individuals, and families for whom formal structured intervention is necessary in order to break through the denial and repression that this disease creates. If the disease has progressed so far that formal structured intervention is necessary for treatment, then all the evidence points to residential treatment as the treatment of choice.

There are many fine outpatient treatment centers throughout the country. However, it has been my experience that if formal intervention is necessary but the individuals are then treated on an outpatient rather than inpatient basis, the success rate for long-term recovery is extremely low.

The alcoholic and addict have met with continued failure. Time and time again they have attempted to adjust, control, manage, and treat their problems on their own. If we undertreat individuals we are setting them up for one more failure, and they may not have the emotional strength to try again. Outpatient treatment works and can be equally as successful as residential treatment. However, in my experience, outpatient treatment is not nearly as successful as residential treatment for patients with whom we have formally intervened.

Choosing a Treatment Facility

This section on selection of a treatment center is designed to help you to be an informed consumer. However, it will not make you an expert in the evaluation of treatment facilities. Do listen to professional recommendations from your interventionist. But, in addition, gather some data for yourself. Remember that the more familiar and the more comfortable you are with the treatment site selected, the more that comfort and confidence will be communicated to your loved one, resulting in an easier intervention.

10

Preparing for the Intervention

To help make the intervention process different from the confrontations of the past, it is important that preparation occur within a structured format. The following intervention preparation worksheets will help. Ample room has been left for you to make notes in the book itself if you desire. However, for purposes of privacy you may wish to do your writing in a separate notebook.

Do not expect to be able to complete these worksheets and to be able to prepare fully for the intervention without the guidance and support of your trained interventionist. I believe that the assistance of a trained interventionist is not only important, but essential.

Worksheets

"_____, I'm here today
(Name)
**because I care about you.
I love you.**"

What is special about this person?

_____

_____

_____

_____

_____

What behaviors and attitudes have you seen that clearly demonstrate the B side of his or her personality?

_____

_____

_____

_____

What endears him or her to you? Remember to be specific.

_____

_____

_____

_____

_____

"But _____, I'm concerned. Do you
(Name)
remember when . . ."

What happened? Be specific; he or she may not remember.

_____

_____

_____

_____

_____

When did it happen?

_____

_____

_____

_____

_____

What did you feel?

_____

_____

_____

_____

_____

Past event (this helps eliminate the excuse that the problems are caused by recent stress and pressure):

_____

_____

_____

_____

_____

Recent event (this helps eliminate the excuse that it is better now, it is under control now):

_____

_____

_____

_____

_____

Choose three other alcohol- or drug-related events that affected you and write about them.

_____

_____

_____

_____

**It is difficult to remember sometimes because
of your own denial and repression.
Here are some tips to help jog your memory.**

If this person is your spouse, what effect has his or her addiction had on your relationship?

Memory triggers:

Birthdays_____

_____

_____

_____

Anniversaries_____

_____

_____

_____

Communication_____

_____

_____

_____

Sexual relationship_____

_____

_____

_____

The children_____

_____

_____

_____

If the person you want to help is your parent, what effect has his or her disease had on you?

Memory triggers:

Your friends_____

_____

_____

_____

Having friends over_____

_____

_____

_____

School events_____

_____

_____

_____

Dates_____

_____

_____

_____

Preparing for the Intervention

Abuse_____

_____

_____

_____

Blame_____

_____

_____

_____

Out-of-control anger_____

_____

_____

_____

What effects have you seen the disease have on your other parent?

_____

_____

_____

_____

_____

How is that parent treated by the addicted parent?

_____

_____

_____

_____

_____

When have you wanted to leave home because of the problem?

_____

_____

_____

_____

_____

What effects on other siblings have you observed?

_____

_____

_____

_____

_____

If the person you are concerned about is an adolescent:
Memory triggers:

Attitude_____

_____

_____

_____

_____

Grades_____

_____

_____

_____

_____

Old peers_____

_____

_____

_____

_____

Choice of new friends_____

_____

_____

_____

_____

Erosion of values_____

_____

_____

_____

Long-range goals_____

_____

_____

_____

_____

If the person you are concerned about is a grandparent:

Memory triggers:

Effect on you_____

_____

_____

_____

_____

Effect on other grandchildren_____

_____

_____

_____

_____

Fear you have of future relationship with your children____

_____

_____

_____

_____

Effect on your siblings_____

_____

_____

_____

_____

Effect on your parents_____

_____

_____

_____

_____

If the person you are concerned about is a friend, what effect has the disease had on your friendship?

Memory triggers:

Your comfort level around your friend_____

_____

_____

_____

_____

Pain you see in his or her family_____

_____

_____

_____

_____

Pain you see in his or her spouse_____

_____

_____

_____

_____

Pain you see in his or her children_____

_____

_____

_____

_____

Have you gotten involved in the addiction by protecting or covering up for your friend?

Ways you have tried to help_____

_____

_____

_____

_____

Do you see your friend less? If so, why?_____

_____

_____

_____

_____

What overall fears have you had for your friend's health and safety?

_____

_____

_____

_____

_____

What excuses is your chemically dependent loved one going to use for not accepting treatment today?

_____

_____

_____

_____

_____

_____

_____

_____

_____

_____

What kinds of replies can you give to each of these excuses?

_____

_____

_____

_____

_____

_____

_____

_____

_____

_____

11

Hope for the First Time

The title of this book was much debated. One idea for the title was "Don't Let Them Die." The reason was simple. Alcohol and drug addiction kill. The book could also have been called "Don't Let America Die."

The most recent statistics available as of March 1989 estimate that one-third of America's workforce is harmfully involved with alcohol or drugs. If each suffering alcoholic and addict impacts directly the lives of at least four other people, who is left in our culture that is not directly affected by this disease?

The dimensions of the negative social impacts of addiction are enormous. For example, the economic loss in the United States as a result of lowered productivity due to addiction is estimated to be $120 billion a year. Added to this is the increased cost of health care as a direct result of this disease, and the tremendous drain that it creates upon our legal system, our jails, and our police. The health-care costs of a cocaine-addicted baby are staggering. Each year 375,000 babies born in the United States are affected by alcohol and other drugs.

In a recent survey, conducted one Sunday in the churches of the state of Oregon, half of those interviewed said someone close to them had an alcohol or drug problem.

I know of no sane person who is not troubled by these statistics and frightened by what is happening to our culture. Yet most of us take no action. We expect someone else to solve the problem. We pressure the schools to have alcohol and drug programs. Now some schools are even doing quasi-treatment, which involves facilitator-led groups before and after school for chemically dependent children. Students often get credit for participation. We become angry and frustrated with our law enforcement officials for not doing a better job of stopping the flow of drugs. We become frustrated with the court system for not keeping drug dealers in jail. We hope against hope that the employer will catch the one we are concerned about and force him or her into treatment. And certainly we believe our government ought to be doing something about it.

But the problem of addiction cannot be solved by government, police, schools, churches, or the court system. The solution has to begin within the family. You are the closest. You have the most information. And above all, you have the power of love.

It is time we as individuals and families stop deluding ourselves and stop hoping that someone else is going to solve the problem for us. Our failure to take action ourselves has caused what used to be a manageable problem to become an epidemic. As a result, we as a culture have been caught up in a web of denial and continue to do exactly what the alcoholic and addict do, which is to redefine what is acceptable and what is normal. I remember well the days not that many years ago when the arrest of someone for possessing or dealing a small amount of drugs made headlines in the paper. Today police are forced to look the other way unless the quantities of drugs involved are extremely large. Recently I was involved in an intervention in which the addict occasionally dealt kilos of cocaine. Law enforcement officials were relatively uninterested in him because they had far bigger fish to fry.

Our attitudes toward drugs have changed. For example, we used to be worried when anyone used cocaine. Then we said, "Well, at least they are not freebasing." Later we said, "At least they are not injecting." Now we are on the verge of saying, "Well, it's just cocaine they're shooting up. Thank God they are not mixing it with heroin, too." We have gone from being concerned about kids in college experimenting with drugs to accepting as a normal part of life that 60 percent of our high-school students experiment with drugs. Junior-high-school officials accept the necessity of dealing with drugs on campus as a normal part of their day.

Not long ago I did an intervention with a young night-shift factory worker. After the completion of her treatment and her return to the work environment, she reported back to me that she and one other person were the only two people on the night shift who were not drinking or using drugs on breaks. There were over ninety people on the night shift.

It used to be that alcoholics and drug addicts tried to protect their jobs by concealing their addictions at work.

Work was the last place where their symptoms would show up. But today, drinking and using mood-altering drugs at work have become routine and accepted behaviors.

At what point does the redefining of what is normal and what is acceptable stop? At what point do we as loved ones stop looking the other way and hoping someone else will act? The alcohol and drug problem in our society today is a cancer in the very fabric of our culture. It is destroying young minds. It is destroying families. It is causing a huge drain on our economy. And it is destroying lives. If our society were a patient in a hospital, the patient would be assessed as being critically ill, placed in intensive care, and probably put on life-support systems.

There are those who will read this book and say that I am an alarmist. But sometimes reality can be quite alarming. As I travel about this country doing interventions, as I have for the past ten years, people ask me what kind of work I do. When I reply, they invariably tell me a story about someone they know and love who has an alcohol or drug problem. Never have I heard someone say, "Gee, I don't know anyone affected by that problem." I long for the day when I do.

If you are reading this book you are probably reading it because someone close to you has an alcohol or drug problem. If so, you are that person's best hope. I encourage you not to look the other way and hope that someone else will intervene. Dare to care. Care enough to try. Care enough to get professional advice. Care enough to reach out. The worst that can happen is that your loved one's addiction will continue. But with professional guidance you have an excellent chance of saving a life and making a friend forever.

If you are a loved one of someone affected with alcohol or drug problems and have gotten this far in the book, you may still be feeling afraid. Know that fear is normal and natural. Remember that it is part of your codependency. Equally, it is a part of our culture. We have had ingrained in us that we ought not to say things which are going to hurt people's feelings. The author John Powell perhaps says it best: "The kindest thing we have to offer one another is the truth."

Yes, what lies ahead of you is scary, but I would ask you to remember that we are talking about an opportunity to save families, to save careers, and to save lives. Remember also that we are talking about intervention, which is not as traumatic as confrontation. Albert Camus, the French philosopher, once said, "We need either to walk through the fear or to succumb to it." Unless you begin acting now, the chances are that you will succumb to it. I encourage you to begin today to start walking through the fear. Go to your telephone book, find the alcohol or drug hotlines, treatment facilities, and interventionists in your community, and make the first telephone call.

From the moment you make that call, you will have started on your own course of recovery and have become part of the solution to the problem of addiction. As you continue on that journey, I wish you Godspeed.

Bibliography

Alcoholics Anonymous World Services, Inc. *Alcoholics Anonymous*. New York, 1976.

Beattie, Melody. *Codependent No More*. New York: Harper/Hazelden, 1987.

———. *Codependents' Guide to the Twelve Steps*. New York: Prentice Hall Press, 1990.

Bradshaw, John. *Bradshaw On: The Family*. Deerfield Beach, Florida: Health Communications, 1988.

———. *Healing the Shame That Binds You*. Deerfield Beach, Florida: Health Communications, 1988.

Burgin, James E. *Guidebook for the Family with Alcohol Problems*. Center City, Minnesota: Hazelden, 1982.

Carnes, Patrick, Ph.D. *Contrary to Love: Helping the Sexual Addict*. Minneapolis, Minnesota: CompCare Publishers, 1989.

———. *Out of the Shadows: Understanding Sexual Addiction*. Minneapolis, Minnesota: CompCare Publishers, 1983.

Gold, Mark S., M.D. *800-Cocaine*. New York: Bantam Books, 1984.

Johnson Institute. *How to Use Intervention in Your Professional Practice*. Minneapolis, Minnesota: Johnson Institute Books, 1987.

Johnson, Vernon, D.D. *I'll Quit Tomorrow*. New York: Harper & Row, 1980.

———. *Intervention*. Minneapolis, Minnesota: Johnson Institute Books, 1986.

Ketcham, Katherine, and Ginny Lyford Gustafson. *Living on the Edge*. New York: Bantam Books, 1989.

McAuliffe, Robert M., Ph.D., and Mary Boesen McAuliffe, Ph.D.

Bibliography

Essentials of Chemical Dependency, Volume 1. Minneapolis, Minnesota: The American Chemical Dependency Society, 1975.

———. *Essentials for the Diagnosis of Chemical Dependency, Volume 2.* Minneapolis, Minnesota: The American Chemical Dependency Society, 1975.

Middelton-Moz, Jane, and Lorie Dwinell. *After the Tears: Reclaiming the Personal Losses of Childhood.* Deerfield Beach, Florida: Health Communications, 1986.

Schaef, Anne Wilson. *Co-Dependence: Misunderstood, Mistreated.* San Francisco: Harper & Row, 1986.

———. *When Society Becomes an Addict.* San Francisco: Harper & Row, 1987.

Strachan, J. George. *Alcoholism: Treatable Illness.* Center City, Minnesota: Hazelden, 1982.

Sullivan, J. Michael, Ph.D., and Katie Evans, C.A.D.C. *Dual Diagnosis: A Guide for Counselors.* New York: Guilford Press, 1989.

Wegscheider-Cruse, Sharon. *Another Chance.* Palo Alto, California: Science and Behavior Books, 1981.